Classroom Discipline: Case Studies and Viewpoints

Second Edition

by
Sylvester Kohut, Jr.

Dale G Range

nea PROFESSIONAL LIBRARY

National Education Association
Washington, D.C.

Note:
The opinions expressed in this publication should not be construed as representing the policy or position of the National Education Association. Materials published as part of the NEA Aspects of Learning series are intended to be discussion documents for teachers who are concerned with specialized interests of the profession.

Previously published material used in this book may use the pronoun "he" to denote an abstract individual, e.g., "the student." We have not attempted to alter this material, although we currently use "she/he" in such instances.

Printing History:
    First printing: January 1979
    Second printing: September 1980
    Third printing: October 1983

    Second Edition: September 1986

Library of Congress Cataloging-in-Publication Data

Kohut, Sylvester, 1942–
    Classroom discipline.

    (NEA aspects of learning)
    Bibliography: p.
    1. Classroom management.   2. School discipline.
I. Range, Dale G   II. Title.   III. Series.
LB3013.K64   1986   371.1'024   86-16176
ISBN 0-8106-1486-3

Contents

The Authors

Dr. Sylvester Kohut, Jr., is Dean, College of Education, Kutztown University, Kutztown, Pennsylvania.

Dr. Dale G Range is Professor of Education and Chair, Department of Elementary, Reading, and Special Education, School of Psychology and Education, Southwest Missouri State University, Springfield, Missouri.

The Consultants

The following educators have reviewed the manuscript and provided helpful comments and suggestions: Joan C. Chapman, Sixth Grade Teacher, Fort Hill Elementary School, Dalton, Georgia; and Carolyn Winningham, Fifth and Sixth Grade Reading Teacher, Pickett County Elementary School, Byrdstown, Tennessee.

Preface to the Second Edition

The second edition of *Classroom Discipline: Case Studies and Viewpoints* is designed to aid teachers in exploring and using the combined values of both the theoretical and practical dimensions of learning. It provides important implications for daily interaction and communication between teachers and pupils in K–12. The text uses a diversity of approaches making it suitable for undergraduate as well as graduate courses, practicums, or as a workshop for an in-service program for teachers and other educators.

The case studies and illustrations included herein are actual, real-life situations observed, recorded, documented, and contributed by teachers, administrators, and paraprofessionals throughout the country. The case studies represent problems and issues common to urban, suburban, and rural school districts and school personnel. The authors' views and opinions are based, in part, on direct experiences as classroom teachers and professors in higher education, serving as consultants to school districts, professional educational organizations, and educational agencies at the federal, state, and regional levels.

The basic purpose of the text is to provide concerned classroom practitioners with a practical guide for understanding and improving classroom management. Ultimately the goal is to enhance that aspect of learning which is so important to teacher and learner alike—*discipline*.

We hope you will find this expanded second edition to be both an action plan and a resource for all segments of the school staff.

CHAPTER 1

Perspectives on Discipline

OVERVIEW

Since early colonial days, essays on teacher training and numerous collections of educational archives on pedagogy have reflected many important issues, but none more controversial or widely debated than classroom discipline and its ramifications for instruction and learning. Discipline has been a concern of classroom practitioners since the days of the one-room schoolhouse and the stern instructor with a hickory switch. In recent times, countless polls and scientific surveys conducted among educators have helped discipline maintain its dubious distinction as the most troublesome issue confronting school personnel. Novice teachers are not the only frustrated group when it comes to classroom discipline, for many well-seasoned and experienced teachers have pleaded that "children are certainly different today because they just don't respect authority." Many pupils, who have little self-respect or self-pride, make it very difficult for teachers or parents to instill genuine respect for any authority figure, especially for the classroom teacher.

Newspapers, magazines, and scholarly publications spotlight topics such as violence in the schools, court decisions on corporal punishment and child abuse, vandalism, terrorism, absenteeism and drug and alcohol addiction. All these popular themes, directly or indirectly, identify discipline in the classroom as a national concern and a serious challenge to educators.

Traditional views of discipline applied to the classroom emphasize that teacher control of pupil behavior is essential for learning. (Mendler & Curwin, 1983) From this standpoint, unless firm control and clear rules are established and continually monitored and enforced, pupils will probably become obstinate and mischievous.

Dubelle and Hoffman (1984) have expressed a more contemporary view of discipline as the development within pupils of the necessary personal controls to allow them to be effective, contributing members of a free society. The Phi Delta Kappa Commission on Discipline (1982) concluded that "The challenge for educators and all adults, then, is to help children develop the skills of responsible behavior by creating an environment in which children may acquire those skills." Both views are humanistic in nature and quite contrary to the traditional "rules to be obeyed" approach.

Both viewpoints, traditional and humanistic, have many supporters today, and continued argumentation between the two camps is ongoing and heated. The controversy is not of recent origin, for at different periods in the history of American public schooling, one view was in vogue while the other struggled for supremacy, or at least acknowledgment. With the advent of the Progressive Education Movement throughout the country, a more humanistic mood toward classroom discipline evolved. This movement, with its more permissive and humanistic self-discipline counterpoint, challenged the traditional view of discipline. Traditionalists attacked many aspects of progressivism, including its "permissive" approach to classroom managment. When the Progressive Education Movement waned and splintered, educators became reactionary and again stressed the 3 Rs. This rejection also meant a reemphasis on more traditional approaches for maintaining classroom order and discipline. In a manner of speaking, there was now a fourth R—"respect"—in the form of strict discipline. By the mid-1960s, when the 3 Rs or 4Rs were again under assault by a new wave of humanists, this also meant the resurgence of a more humane approach to discipline. According to the humanists, a discipline code depicted as forcing conformity, degrading pupils, and discriminatory toward minority group learners was intolerable.

During this period a deluge of best-selling hardback and paperback books dealing with these issues flooded the market, greatly influencing public thought as well as public school decision making. Some of the more influential books were Neill's *Summerhill*

(1960), Goodman's *Compulsory Mis-Education* (1962), Conant's *Slums and Suburbs* (1961), Holt's *How Children Fail* (1964), Kozol's *Death at an Early Age* (1967), Kohl's *Thirty-six Children* (1968), Glasser's *Schools Without Failure* (1969), Kohl's *The Open Classroom* (1969), and Silberman's *Crisis in the Classroom* (1970). Proposed models for open education, free schools, and other alternative systems of schooling and classroom learning demanded educational reforms and new approaches to classroom communication.

A major thrust in education today is to return to the basics. Critics have attributed the student unrest and violence of the 1960s, the rapid decline in SAT scores, and the increased turmoil in the schools to the "permissiveness" of the humanistic backlash of the past decade. There is, in addition, an apparent concern, however, that current pressures for the "back-to-basics" movement might be misinterpreted by many administrators, teachers, and parents as also inferring the need for a rapid return to a more traditional stand on discipline. This would be a serious error!

In the midst of this give-and-take many classroom teachers, some of whom were among the student ranks of the 1960s, have remained confused, unsure, and frustrated while searching for standards or guidelines that work. Many agree, at least in concept, that student self-discipline is the best way. But in the real world of the classroom, they have encountered disruptive behavior, militant students, and a feeling of utter helplessness. Teachers who abandoned rules soon discovered chaos. Teachers who established and tried to enforce strict rules soon found hostility and rebellion.

Is there a philosophical compromise position on discipline for the classroom teacher to espouse and implement? What techniques really are effective? Will emphasizing a middle-ground position be construed as wishy-washy? How can educators incorporate the best elements of both approaches—traditional and humanistic—in an effort to establish reliable classroom management techniques?

It is the contention of the authors that certain aspects of both the traditional and the humanistic views can be interwoven into a scheme which will provide the teacher with successful strategies and practices for maximizing learning and minimizing disruptive behaviors in the classroom setting. All social groups and subgroups establish and maintain rules and regulations which apply to all members of the respective groups. The authors submit that in a classroom specific rules and regulations governing pupil behavior can provide the necessary structure without offsetting efforts to create a social-emotional climate conducive to student self-discipline. The traditional and humanistic views are not mutually exclusive. There can be general compatibility between them. Teachers can establish guidelines and use practices which minimize disruptive behaviors and at the same time help students to develop self-discipline. To accomplish this Herculean task, an understanding of the causes and consequences of disruptive behavior is a prerequisite.

Sound techniques based on the latest research findings as well as good, old-fashioned, practical experiences will enable the teacher to achieve this dual objective. Disruptive behaviors in the classroom will be minimized and student self-discipline maximized if the teacher is able to successfully demonstrate 1) effective instructional procedures; 2) an understanding of the pupil's physical, psychological, emotional, and social needs; 3) appropriate techniques for helping the learner cope with change, stress, and self-identification; 4) an understanding of the special needs of the culturally different and culturally disadvantaged student; 5) proven skills, techniques, and strategies for successful classroom communication.

DEFINITION

Unlike practitioners in other professions, educators usually find it difficult, if not impossible, to agree upon specific definitions of common terms and practices. In the medical profession, the term *myocardial infarction* which means "heart attack" is rarely misunderstood by a nurse or doctor. In a court of law, every attorney and judge understands that *tort* means "a wrongful act, injury or damage which does not involve a breach of contract for which a civil action can be brought." But in the field of education, if you ask a group of forty teachers to define or explain the meaning of *individualized instruction* or *behavioral objective,* you will probably get forty different and conflicting interpretations. Attempting to gain a general consensus for a definition of *discipline* among educators is a confounding task.

Webster's *New World Dictionary* defines *discipline* as "training that develops self-control, character, orderliness and efficiency," "accepting of or submission to authority and control," and "a system of rules or methods, as for the conduct of members of a monastic order." Webster defines *to discipline* "to develop by instruction and exercise." Discipline is teaching and learning; it is *not* punishment. Discipline is two-dimensional, for it involves both *imposed* and *self-discipline*. What is your definition of *discipline*? Does it differ from that of your colleagues and students?

There are educators who believe that discipline is synonymous with classroom management. They say that a well-planned lesson is the best deterrent to a noisy and disruptive classroom. Unfortunately, many teachers are judged on their ability to keep a class quiet; this is the sole criterion for their evaluation. It is inconceivable that learning is restricted only to a "quiet" and orderly classroom. However, supervisors usually endorse a "lively" classroom atmosphere but often resort to measuring a teacher's ability in terms of the lowest readings on the imaginary gauge that registers the classroom sound level in decibels!

Classroom management is an all-encompassing term which refers to virtually every facet of interaction and activity—planned and spontaneous—which may occur in an academic classroom, science laboratory, or gymnasium. The meaning of *discipline,* on the other hand, is narrow; it infers self-respect and respect for other persons. There are teachers who are reluctant to take any redirective action, even when warranted, against a disobedient pupil because such action might seem to be an admission of failure or might subject the teacher to ridicule from unkind colleagues. On the contrary, it is often more of an injustice to the pupil not to initiate any action. On occasion, such action might mean isolating the pupil from the classroom setting. There are boys and girls who honestly cannot function in a classroom situation and who require special counseling, psychological or psychiatric referral. There is no shame in admitting that such a situation exists and requesting help.

Students have their own unwritten definitions of discipline. Because of a driving need to please the peer group and for other reasons, any type of attention from teacher or classmates is a form of positive reinforcement in the minds of some pupils. Knowingly violating a major or minor school regulation in front of a teacher is a silent message that the pupil is seeking attention from the teacher. It is inconsequential to the student that the attention may take the form of a scolding or after-school detention for misbehavior. Teachers often unconsciously reward these undesired or inappropriate behaviors which may often be the self-satisfying goal of the pupil. Children quite normally seek affection and acceptance from teachers and peers. When the thirst for affection and attention becomes excessive or abnormal, however, teachers should be alert. Even conscientious educators daydreaming about their early school days can recall the name of the class clown. The clown would act out our wildest caprice or prank on the teacher or other classmates, for we feared punishment or reprisal. After a while the clown began to accept his/her role, and what evolved was a case of a self-fulfilling prophecy.

Most institutions of higher learning today employ a small army of well-trained specialists who use every known technique to help undergraduates and graduates cope with the emotional adjustments and traumas of everyday life on the campus. Techniques range from traditional counseling and group therapy sessions to sophisticated laboratory experimentation in biofeedback. Their objective is to reduce anxiety and depression and help students relax, with the ultimate aim of improving academic achievement in the classroom. Because of financial restraints and general skepticism of new methods untested on youngsters, educators in basic education have been reluctant to hire extra counselors with special training. Therefore, as an alternative, there is a definite need for classroom teachers to assume a proactive role in dealing with certain communication and interpersonal encounters related, among other things, to discipline. Wayson and Lasley (1984) stress that rules for classroom and in-school behavior must go beyond merely being printed and distributed. Rules must be taught. The "best" rules are those that are the products of wide discussion and acceptance.

Defining *discipline* in the classroom is the first stage in establishing a school-wide program. Discipline is a process involving teachers, parents, and students. An effective program for classroom management and discipline should stress student awareness and self-discipline. While there may certainly be different solutions or approaches suitable for a particular situation, it is of paramount importance that the approach selected facilitate the ongoing academic experiences of *all* students in the class. The approach selected should provide for a positive rather than a punitive or negative confrontation between teacher and pupil whenever possible. The approach selected should be compatible with the personality, teaching style, and educational philosophy of the teacher.

REGIONALISM

Are certain discipline problems especially unique to teachers in different locations such as rural, suburban, and urban school districts? Does the psychological profile of the typical student enrolled in a rural school district differ from that of the typical student enrolled in a suburban or urban school district? Are similar discipline problems treated differently in various parts of the country? These are crucial questions worthy of exploration.

Regardless of geographic region, classroom discipline and its effect on learning are common concerns of all administrators and teachers. (Gallup 1985) It is difficult to generalize about a particular region or student subpopulation. Just as there are distinct life-styles and backgrounds represented in any classroom, so are there distinct commonalities among the student body. In all schools the principal is the educational leader who sets the tone for any formal or informal disciplinary code or regulation. As there is no one best instructional pattern which will ensure success in the classroom, so there is no one best approach in dealing with disciplinary cases. In any learning environment, the teacher needs to be cognizant of and ready to use a variety of proven methods and techniques.

Rural Profile. There are observable differences among rural, suburban, and urban youth, just as there are observable differences among rural, suburban, and urban teachers. Rural people are generally conservative. Religion is an important ingredient in everyday life, and family ties are strong. Rural children learn very early to assume responsibilities on the farm and at home. They are expected to perform chores and special jobs just like any other member of the family. (Welch 1976) Absenteeism from school during important planting and harvesting seasons is routine in farming communities. The first day of the large and small game hunting season may be an unofficial holiday. Because of absenteeism and limited cultural experiences, rural boys and girls tend to lag behind urban and suburban students in almost all academic subjects as measured by standardized tests. (Gilligan 1974) Most rural children are taught to display respect for elders and authority with infractions readily and swiftly punished at home. Since the same attitude of obedience is common in the schools, rural parents generally support or encourage corporal punishment. (Phelps 1984) If something is amiss in school, it is not uncommon for a parent or guardian to confront the teacher or school officials.

The dropout rate in rural communities is extremely high; in some Appalachian regions it is about 65 percent. Because many children are encouraged to remain on the farm or seek employment in nonskill mill or factory jobs, many parents see little worth in schooling beyond the junior high school years. Recent innovations in curriculum engineering and the introduction of vocational-technical and agricultural programs have helped reduce the dropout rate in some communities. Consolidation of rural school districts has alleviated some problems but, in turn, has created new problems. (Phelps 1984) It is not uncommon for rural children to spend hours traveling to and from school by bus. The long distances between clusters of farmhouses and the regional or community school present a serious transportation problem. After-school activities are difficult to establish and maintain because of the logistical and financial problems associated with rural school settings. In addition, family incomes in many isolated rural areas are far below federal poverty guidelines. As a result, proper health care and adequate food for the children are never-ending concerns of school personnel. A considerable number of one-room schoolhouses and totally dilapidated school buildings without indoor running water or toilet facilities are still in use. The problems of the rural poor are not rapidly on the mend. (Bellon, Doak, and Handler 1979)

Urban Profile. Overcrowding, diverse ethnic minority groups, and the social ills that plague all large metropolitan communities are also reflected in the urban schools. Federally funded programs like Talent Search and Project Upward Bound are designed to identify and assist academically able secondary school pupils and to provide remedial, developmental, cultural, and recreational activities with the express intent of keeping potentially productive students in school. These programs eventually aim at assisting such students in gaining admission to post-secondary institutions. Federal programs also help to supplement state and local service projects which try to assist all needy students—rural, suburban, and urban.

Every crime or injustice found in the streets of the big cities may be found in the hallways and corridors of most big city schools. In addition, teacher turnover is extremely high, thus causing a great deal of instability in academic programs. Low self-esteem and constant peer-group pressure may confuse and confound even the most willing and able learners. If there is no discipline and mutual respect in the classroom, and if the child is never encouraged at home, positive reinforcement and praise from the teacher in school may seem merely like another "do-gooder" action trying to get through to an unwilling learner. Rebellion in the streets may soon become rebellion in the school. While big cities attempt to rebuild, the rebuilding of the public school system takes a low priority. City school enrollments have declined substantially since 1970 with "white flight" to the suburbs, even though Black and Spanish-speaking student populations are rapidly increasing. Between 1980 and 1985 the number of families headed by a single female increased 41 percent. While many cities are not experiencing increased growth in total population during the 1980s, the percentage of the poor and needy continues to increase at a fast and uncontrollable rate. Rural poor continue to move into the cities seeking employment, and the rural child is thrust into the public school system. The implications of these changes for public schools are overwhelming! (Kozol 1985)

Suburban Profile. The American dream of living in suburbia in a split-level home with two cars in the driveway has become a reality for millions of middle- and upper-middle-class families. The fastest growing community group in the United States is suburban. In 1980, for example, more people lived in suburban complexes than in either cities or rural communities. The flight to the "country" has resulted in a massive overbuilding of schools. With the declining birthrate, however, many boom-period schools of the 1950s, 1960s, and 1970s, are now being closed. Even today, well-meaning parents may ask the realtor about the "school situation" before signing a mortgage on their dream house in the suburbs. Suburban schools, however, are far from being the "dream" imagined by parents. Affluent middle- and upper-middle-class children are burdened with many problems and frustrations similar to those of their city cousins. There is a conscious effort to rebel against traditional middle-class values. Pressures for good grades and an admission ticket to a "good" college among academically minded students lead to cheating and even more dangerous acts. Drugs are no longer the private domain of the ghetto dweller, and most suburban schools are confronted daily with a wide array of vandalism, vices, and petty crimes.

According to Toffler's *Learning for Tomorrow*, we live in a transient society, and our schools must assume a leadership role in preparing youth for change. There is a vital need to establish and maintain communication lines with all students at all times. This must be a shared responsibility among all participants in educational communities throughout the country.

VIOLENCE

In the New York City high school where *Blackboard Jungle* was filmed in 1955, a teacher was beaten by students so severely that he now suffers impaired vision from a blow with a belt buckle. In Los Angeles, a group of high school girls, angry over low grades, set a female teacher's hair afire. In San Francisco, an elementary teacher was beaten and raped in front of the screaming students in her classroom by a couple of high school boys. In rural Missouri, an upset third grader twisted a teacher's thumb and tore several ligaments in her hand. In Philadelphia, a social studies teacher on the way to his car after school, was shot to death by a drunken student. The son of a prominent family in Austin, Texas, fatally shot his high school English teacher in the classroom because the boy was upset over low grades and being the brunt of the teacher's jokes during class. In affluent Huntingdon Valley, Pennsylvania, a second-grader, on her way to the library to pick up materials for her teacher, was raped in the hallway by an intruder. In such an atmosphere, many threats, as well as sexual harassment of women teachers, often go unreported because of real or imagined fear of reprisal or shame in public disclosure of embarrassing incidents. In some areas, there are media reports of the sensationalism of violent crimes in the schools; in other towns and cities, there is censorship or cover-up of such violence.

In 1977, Memphis school officials reported 680 assaults, 144 of which were directed against teachers or administrators; Miami officials registered 1,153 attacks; and Boston schools recorded 155 assaults on teachers. In the New York City and Chicago public schools, a combined total of over 4,200 attacks was reported. (*Time*,

23 January 1978; and *Safe School Study.)* This rapid increase in violent crimes and acts in public schools pits student against student, student against teacher, and outsider against both student and teacher. To offset this increase in violent crimes, many schools throughout the country have become armed camps with specially trained security guards who roam corridors and check restrooms, closed-circuit television monitors, emergency classroom telephones, security entrance checkpoints, and stiff enforcement of student and staff identification card regulations. In New York City, teacher assault cases are now prosecuted by legal departments rather than educational agencies and officials. The emotional and psychological strains are so damaging that in Los Angeles and New York, battered-teacher groups coordinated by a psychiatric consultant have been established.

The following experience illustrates many of the problems which teachers encounter. Richard Weinstein was graduated in 1975 from Temple University in Philadelphia and immediately accepted a faculty appointment in the Harrisburg City School District. Although enthusiastic and committed to a teaching career, two years later he quit! A few days after resigning, Weinstein wrote an emotional letter to the editor of the *Harrisburg Evening News.* When published, the letter caused a stir among teachers. As one teacher remarked, "I am glad the letter appeared. Now the public is getting a chance to see what really goes on in the schools." The young teacher's letter recounted the violence and verbal abuse teachers are subjected to daily. He was critical of the district's discipline code which he said was ineffective and unenforceable. This particular policy was just beginning to be implemented when Weinstein resigned. (Harrisburg School District Code of Conduct) Although he was a beginning teacher, Weinstein insisted that it was not "culture shock" that forced his resignation, since he had attended public school in Harrisburg and did his student teaching in a tough Philadelphia ghetto high school. He claimed that 70 to 80 percent of his time in the classroom was spent trying to keep kids under control. "I taught in an open space middle school, and that alone prohibits any real teaching from going on. There were kids running in the corridors constantly, throwing erasers and pencils, smoking cigarettes and dope, and yelling and screaming. Whenever a fight broke out in another area, everyone somehow got involved in it," he commented.

Weinstein noted that there was a knife attack in the school; he had heard about an eighth grader who was found with a gun on his person, and saw detectives lead another student away from the school in handcuffs. "A student who threw a chair at me was suspended for three days and allowed to return. During the three-day suspension period, he managed to get arrested for shoplifting and purse snatching." The former teacher believes that alternative learning centers for discipline problems are nothing more than glorified playgrounds where very little takes place and habitual offenders are able to regroup for the next assault or infraction. Weinstein suggested that prospective teachers be better prepared in the psychology of the classroom and in dealing with emotional and disruptive behavioral problems; that pre-service and in-service training include establishing better communication networks with parents and guardians.

After his experiences as a middle school teacher, what will Weinstein do now? "I'm lucky because I'm young and single. I can pick up and leave a bad situation. I know teachers who feel the same way but are tied to the problem because they're trying to raise a family and pay the bills. I need to get away from teaching. I was told that I was a good teacher. Someday I'd like to get involved with kids again, but in a different way and in a different atmosphere."

According to the media, discipline problems and violence are often as much a part of schooling as reading, writing, and arithmetic. In 1976 the National Education Association (NEA) Research department conducted a scientific nationwide survey which dealt with many issues, including school discipline. (*Today's Education*, September/October 1976) The greatest proportion of teachers reported that two factors, irresponsible parents and unsatisfactory home conditions, were responsible to a great extent or to some extent for misbehavior in public schools. The figures were 85.8 and 80.0 percent respectively for both factors. Next, teachers cited the following items to a great degree or to some degree responsible: overcrowded classes, 55.9 percent; irrelevant school curriculum which did not meet needs of students, 45.7 percent; lack of programming for exceptional students, 45.5 percent; and lack of authority by teachers to determine or mete out punishment, 45.4 percent. A sample of selected additional crucial items follows.

	Widespread or frequent	Present, but not widespread or frequent	Rarely occurs	Never occurs
Impertinence and discourtesy to teachers	29.1	50.2	20.0	.8
Theft (small items of little value)	28.6	53.0	17.7	.6
Destruction of school property	23.7	48.3	24.6	3.5
Theft (serious nature: money, etc.)	13.7	46.6	35.5	4.1
Carrying dangerous weapons	2.8	17.4	51.8	27.9
Assault on teachers	1.0	7.5	37.1	54.3
Rape	.3	1.4	11.9	86.4

In 1978, the Department of Health, Education, and Welfare and the National Institute of Education released the *Safe School Study* which had been requested by Congress in legislation passed in 1974. The major purpose of the investigation was to determine the nature and extent of school-based crime and violence occurring throughout the country. Among the study's findings, one of the strongest factors in reducing school violence appears to be the principal's leadership. The report notes that approximately 25 percent of American schools suffer from moderately severe to severe problems of vandalism, personal attacks, and thievery. Some estimates of property damage and loss due to vandalism are as high as $600 million yearly. The study does not differentiate among urban, surburban, and rural incidents of personal violence, but it does provide guidelines and implications. Five major findings are outlined as follows:

1. *Location of Serious Problems.* In large urban complexes, 26 percent of the high schools, 18 percent of the junior high schools, and approximately 12 percent of the elementary schools indicate that serious problems are commonplace. About 6 percent of the rural, 8 percent of the suburban, and 11 percent of the small city schools also report serious recurring problems.

2. *Use of Security Officers.* Over 50 percent of big city junior high schools have professional security officers in the schools, and over 65 percent of high schools in the metropolitan areas employ security guards. In suburban schools the number drops to 7 percent, and in rural schools less than 1 percent employ guards.

3. *Hostility Against Teachers.* Considering the entire country, junior high school pupils display more hostility toward their teachers. About 75 percent of urban junior high teachers and about 60 percent of urban senior high teachers report that students swore or made obscene gestures at them in a one-month period. This compares with 40 percent for rural teachers and 48 percent for suburban secondary school teachers.

4. *Teacher Attacks.* The risk of an urban school teacher being attacked is 1 in 55. The risk of a rural teacher being attacked is 1 in 500. Whereas 1.8 percent of all large city secondary school teachers report being attacked in a period of one month, only 0.2 percent of all rural teachers reported attacks.

5. *Student Violence.* The risk of attacks requiring medical attention, and risk of being robbed of items over $10 value is twice as high in schools with fewer than 40 percent white pupils than in schools with more than 70 percent white pupils.

The *Safe School Study* developed a profile of a "safe" school, that is, a school with a low crime rate.

Throughout this analysis, the data point to the principal and the school administration as the key element. An effective principal who has developed a systematic policy of discipline helps each individual teacher to maintain discipline by providing a reliable system of support, appropriate in-service training for teachers, and opportunities for teachers to coordinate their actions. This means that the teachers themselves are in a more secure position and are more likely to take effective disciplinary actions to control their own classrooms. Teachers are also more likely to recognize that they have a responsibility in establishing schoolwide discipline. Students will respond favorably when this occurs; they will see the system as fair, will understand better what the rules are, and will be less likely to feel that the school is capricious and despotic. The effective school also finds ways to provide positive incentives to all students. The honors of the school go to many students, regardless of social class or academic ability. The school is sufficiently comprehensive to offer something of value to all of its students. (*Safe School Study*, p. 137)

While the report indicates that violence in the classroom is primarily a big city problem, it is also a concern in the suburban and rural setting. We live in a violent society and a turbulent time in the history of humankind. The increasing crime rate in our public and private schools must be stopped. While no panacea is proposed in this publication, definite preventive and positive classroom actions and practices are suggested which are worthy of consideration.

CORPORAL PUNISHMENT

"Spare the rod and spoil the child" is an old saying and an old-fashioned justification for the use of corporal punishment in the schools. In most states, policies regarding its use are determined by the local public school district. Perhaps no question during the past twenty years has agitated the public mind more than the subject of corporal punishment in families and in schools. Almost all persons have taken sides on the issue as their practices or prejudices have influenced or swayed their minds. The fact that so much has been said and written, often "in bitterness of speech," as to the use of corporal punishment as a means of moral discipline, both in the past and as presently administered, is positive proof that the expediency and propriety of its use are doubted by many educators.

Some advocates of the "rod," as a means of moral discipline have quoted from the *Bible*, especially the Proverbs of Solomon. (Prov. 13:24, 12:15, 23:13)

While discussing the "Means and Objectives of Common School Education" before the Massachusetts Board of Education in 1837, Horace Mann lectured on the "Subject of Penal Discipline Especially Discipline by Corporal Punishment":

> That corporal punishment, considered by itself, and without reference to its ultimate object, is an evil, probably none will deny. Yet, with almost three thousand public schools in this State, composed of all kinds of children, with more than five thousand teachers, of all grades of qualification, to govern them, probably the evils of corporal punishment must be endured, or the greater ones of insubordination and mutiny be incurred. . . . I cannot, however, forbear to express the opinion, that punishment should never be inflicted, except in cases of the extremest necessity; while the experiment of sympathy, confidence, persuasion, encouragement, should be repeated, for ever and ever. (Mann, pp. 45–46)

Lyman Cobb in 1847 boldly criticized the use of corporal punishment in the home and school when he listed his objections and recommendations for practical substitutions and preventives in his book *On Corporal Punishment.* Cobb's objections and recommended solutions are as relevant and controversial today as they were more than one hundred years ago. Among his more pertinent arguments are the following:

OBJECTIONS TO THE USE OF THE ROD

No parent or teacher knows, when he commences, how long or how severely he must punish a boy before he will yield.

When a boy does not readily yield to the flogging inflicted on him, the parent or teacher generally becomes angry.

Because few, very few children ever do wrong for the sake of doing wrong as such.

Because parents and teachers, when impatient or in anger, very often punish their children or pupils for a trifling matter.

Because parents and teachers very often whip their children or pupils in anger or under excitement, when the anger or excitement has not been produced by the crime or offence.

Because parents and teachers who are in the constant habit of whipping their children or pupils are very apt to be equally severe for unintentional as for intentional wrongs.

Because it very frequently, if not always, produces physical injury to the child on whom it is inflicted.

It is an indirect system of giving a PREMIUM for LYING, particularly when the anticipated whipping has been preceded by THREATENING.

Because it is very often inflicted in consequence of the representations of others; or, by the system of informers.

Because it DESTROYS OR PREVENTS the greater part of the enjoyment and pleasure which should exist between parents and children, and between teachers and pupils.

Because, nine times in ten, the least guilty are detected and punished for the violation of school regulations or other improper or mischievous conduct.

Because when children or pupils leave their home or school, they are to be REASONED with, not whipped or BEATEN.

Because it almost always produces REVENGEFUL feelings on the part of the child or pupil.

SUBSTITUTES AND/OR PREVENTIVES
AND THE USE OF THE ROD

Every parent or teacher should ALWAYS speak kindly and affectionately to his child or pupil.

Every parent or teacher should ALWAYS speak mildly and gently to his child or pupil.

All parents and teachers should endeavor ALWAYS to govern their children or pupils by love rather than by fear.

Every parent and teacher should have patience in all his intercourse with his children or pupils.

Parents and teachers should endeavor ALWAYS to be cheerful and pleasant when in the presence of their children or pupils.

All parents and teachers should remember that, in governing and disciplining children or pupils, persuasion is far better than force.

Parents and teachers should appeal to the SYMPATHIES and BETTER FEELINGS of their children or pupils when they do anything wrong thoughtlessly or intentionally.

All parents and teachers should, by all suitable and proper means within their power, interest and engage the minds of their children or pupils.

Children or pupils should ALWAYS be employed, either usefully or innocently.

Parents and teachers should ALWAYS speak encouragingly to their children or pupils, relative to their efforts, studies, or lessons, or in whatever else they may be engaged.

Parents and teachers should always speak well of, or approve of the good acts which their children or pupils have done, in the presence of friends, or of the school; but they should never speak of, or condemn the faults of their children before others.

Parents and teachers should always have decision and firmness, in all their intercourse, with their children or pupils.

Every parent and teacher should, by all suitable and proper means, endeavor to gain the confidence of his children or pupils.

The teacher should first establish order in his school, before proceeding to any business whatever.

Parents and teachers should require their children or pupils to attend school regularly and punctually.

Parents and teachers should always be just in all their intercourse with their children or pupils.

All parents and teachers should ALWAYS teach and encourage their children to speak the truth.

Parents and teachers should teach their children and pupils to think.

Parents and teachers should deeply impress on the minds of their children and pupils the great importance of self-respect.

Children and pupils should early form the habit and obtain the power of complete and full self-control.

All parents and teachers should teach their children and pupils to be polite and attentive, particularly to those who are aged or infirm, or those older than themselves.

Parents and teachers should constantly impress on the minds of their children and pupils the imperative NECESSITY as well as DUTY strictly to regard NEATNESS and CLEANLINESS, both of dress and person.

Parents and teachers should ALWAYS, in the instruction or education of their children or pupils, appeal to their conscientious sense of right and duty.

Parents should respect and encourage their teachers.

Parents and teachers should always remember that children and pupils have RIGHTS, as well as parents and teachers.

All parents and teachers should encourage their children or pupils to acknowledge the faults, errors, or offenses which they have committed, and thereby make them fully sensible of their responsibility, as children or pupils.

Parents and teachers should continually feel and appreciate the very great responsibility which rests on them, as parents or teachers, in the education, government, and control of their children or pupils.

Corporal punishment was banned throughout France in 1887. Both the USSR and Poland supported the inclusion of a ban on spanking in the schools as part of a declaration of children's rights by the United Nations Commission on Human Rights. In the United States, Maine, Maryland, Massachusetts, and New Jersey actually prohibit corporal punishment in the public schools. In many states where corporal punishment is not specifically prohibited, local school boards often prohibit or severely restrict its use. In California, Delaware, Pennsylvania, and Texas, permission to paddle a child is based on the old common law principal *in loco parentis*. Under this doctrine, the school staff is justified in using any measure that parents or guardians could legally use to discipline the child. Gradually *in loco parentis* is being replaced by state statutes and constitutional principles that establish guidelines for regulations governing pupil classroom and school behavior. Many school districts, with assistance and guidance from professional organizations, have established a student bill of rights program. These documents usually include a broad and comprehensive treatment of student behavior for both in-class and out-of-class activities and situations. For example, regulations may cover student conduct during participation in organized extracurricular enterprises including school-sponsored publications, drama groups, and athletic teams.

Regardless of the code of conduct or rules established, they must adhere to rules of law as determined by the courts and written in light of the current status of state and federal litigation on constitutional issues. (Moriarity 1986)

The following frequently heard arguments in support of corporal or physical punishment in the schools were listed in a National Education Association special *Report of the Task Force on Corporal Punishment* published in 1972:

- Some schools offer no other resources for discipline.
- It's the only thing some kids understand.
- Teachers have to be protected.
- Sometimes a teacher gets so frustrated he just has to hit students.
- Students learn self-discipline from corporal punishment.
- Corporal punishment builds "character" or "masculinity."
- Corporal punishment is no worse than sustained psychological humiliation.
- It makes students feel secure, because they have firm guidance.
- Parents want schools to use it.
- Students want corporal punishment.

The same NEA report listed the following reasons used by some people to justify certain circumstances for the infliction of corporal punishment as well as limited or conditional corporal punishment:

- It's a last resort.
- Parents' permission is required.
- It's very limited in severity.
- It's only used after a thorough procedure.
- Only certain people are authorized to administer corporal punishment.
- It's prescribed only for those individuals who will profit from it.
- It's used on boys only.
- It has to be made legal so it can be used as a deterrent.

CHAPTER 2

Discipline: Theory, Research, and Practice

We contend that many disruptive behaviors can be alleviated before they become serious discipline problems that must then be dealt with by the classroom teacher. Disruptive behaviors will also be greatly reduced by the teacher's ability to employ effective organizational, planning, and instructional procedures. Once classroom control has been established, an analysis of student needs and behaviors will indicate approaches and techniques that the teacher will want to utilize in helping students develop self-discipline and increase their personal growth.

GETTING OFF TO A GOOD START

Practices for minimizing discipline problems should begin on the first day of class. Webster (1968) has appropriately defined this first encounter of student and teacher as the "honeymoon period." During this initial phase when students formulate their impressions of the teacher and the classroom atmosphere, beginning teachers are often misled. Students sit quietly, raise their hands to respond, pay attention, and are generally quite well behaved. The new teacher is easily led to believe that this is an ideal class—a group of "angels." In phase two, some of the angels change. The alteration can occur at anytime during the first week or two. Students begin to test their initial impressions about the teacher and what they "can get away with." Class assignments are not finished, students begin talking to each other, gum chewing appears, and a host of other disruptive behaviors are likely to occur. Webster identifies the third phase as "the period of accommodation or final adjustment." In this phase the effective teacher will be in control of the classroom setting and able to develop maximum learning opportunities for students. The ineffective teacher will be engaged in a "running battle" with students in an attempt to maintain some degree of classroom control and order. Student learning in this situation will be more accidental than developmental.

Research findings and the experiences of successful teachers have identified certain initial practices that seem to minimize disruptive student behaviors and maximize the establishment of an effective learning environment.

Learn School Policies. Prior to meeting a class for the first time, the teacher should become familiar with school policies concerning appropriate student behavior and permissible and suggested disciplinary procedures. She/he should definitely know what the school expects from both student and teacher in regard to discipline. With this information in hand, the teacher is ready to begin planning for the "honeymoon period."

Establish Rules. First, establish a set of classroom rules to guide the behavior of students. If "rules" sound too harsh, use "guidelines." With younger students, rules should be rather general and pertain to behaviors such as paying attention, respect for others, excessive noise, securing materials. With older students, rules can be more specific. In both cases, however, do not overwhelm the student with an excessive number of regulations. The rationale for each rule should be presented to students, and the teacher should ensure that they understand and see a need for each rule. Later, as students become more self-directed, the teacher might allow for modifications if there seems to be a need. However, any changes should be made after the teacher has established control.

Rita Jackson was recently employed to teach a self-contained fifth-grade class. Prior to the beginning of the school year, she read the school policies concerning appropriate student behavior and discipline. In addition, she met with her principal and discussed accepted discipline procedures. She also visited the classroom and noted aspects of the room that might require a rule or guideline. She observed that students kept materials in metal lockers in the rear of the classroom. On the first day of class, Rita had listed on a large piece of posterboard, displayed in a prominent place, those texts and supplies that she wanted students to take to their desks for the morning's work. For the afternoon a similar list was displayed. During the first few days of school, a few students had to return to their lockers for text or supplies they had forgotten. By the end of the week, however, transitions from one subject area to another moved quickly and quietly. No disturbances or wasted time resulted from students returning to their lockers.

Discuss Expectations. Within the first few days or class sessions, inform students what will be expected of them. Letting students know what you will require them to do in class, what you hope to achieve, and how the class will operate helps reduce student tension and confusion. Providing a daily schedule that is followed regularly will give younger children a sense of security and a knowledge of what to expect next. Older students may be provided unit outlines or schedules. It is also important that the teacher explain the goals and purposes of the class and the obligations of both student and teacher in making the class a constructive and rewarding experience.

Jane Carter has a policy of discussing her expectations with each of her seventh-grade English classes. She lists on a large posterboard the goals of the class, what she expects of students, and what students can expect of her. These expectations are discussed at the beginning of the year, and students are encouraged to discuss, question, and/or recommend additions to any category. Periodically throughout the year the categories are reviewed and discussed.

Overplan Lessons. A third initial practice is to "overplan" lessons for the first week or two. The teacher will want to impress upon students from the very beginning that she/he is organized and has "all bases covered." What the teacher does during the first week or two will help establish student expectations of what she/he values and expects from them.

Bill Brown is a third-grade teacher. School policies require that parents furnish paper, pencil, crayons, and scissors for their children. Based on experience, Mr. Brown realizes that not all students have these supplies during the first few days of class. Some parents forget or are waiting for a payday. Some students accidentally or purposely forget their materials, especially on the first day. Since Mr. Brown has specific assignments starting with the first session, he has developed his own set of supplies. During the first few days when an assignment is made and a student replies, "I forgot my crayons, can I share with Allen?" Mr. Brown is there quickly to supply crayons. He finds that this practice minimizes disruptions and problems caused by sharing and borrowing. The student provides Mr. Brown with a written IOU for one box of crayons.

Learn Names. The practice of devising a seating arrangement whereby student names are learned quickly is desirable. Many teachers suggest an alphabetical seating arrangement since it lends itself to associating names with faces. After student names are learned, other seating arrangements can be utilized. Calling a student by name early in the year, however, gives him/her an increased sense of well-being. The student is now a person rather than just a member of the class. Early use of names also gives students the impression that the teacher is organized and in control of the situation. "John and Harold, stop talking and finish your work" is much more effective for John and Harold than "Let's stop talking and finish our work."

Be Firm and Consistent. Experienced educators recommend that teachers begin the year with confidence in self, firmness in dealing with students, and consistency in dealing with disruptive behaviors. Webster (1968) warns teachers not to wear their feelings on their sleeves. Many, especially beginning teachers, view acts of misbehavior as directed to them personally. One who realizes that such behaviors might be reactions to other factors or to the teacher's role rather than to the teacher personally will be in a better position to handle the situation.

Firmness implies using an emphatic voice, looking at the student, and, if necessary, moving toward the student. Firmness also means "sticking by your guns." Many teachers have heard students say, "Well, Mrs. Jones let us do it." A smile and "That's fine; however, in this class you will not do it" demonstrates firmness. Many teachers report that it is easier to begin in a firm manner and relax later in the year than to begin relaxed and then try to become firm.

We would like to emphasize, however, that firmness *does not* mean harshness. A teacher can be firm and still be friendly, supportive, and warm with students. A firm teacher can provide an environment where students feel safe and secure, and feel "This teacher really cares about me."

Consistency in dealing with disruptive behavior is important if students are to judge the teacher fair, not partial. Make sure that the punishment fits the crime and that partiality is not shown to certain students.

Deal with Disruptive Behavior. In addition to firmness and consistency, teacher experience and research recommend additional procedures when dealing with disruptive behavior, including the following:

1. Avoid making the punishment or reprimand personal. Rather than saying that George is bothering you, state that he is disrupting the class or interfering with an activity. If George feels he is bothering you, the behavior may recur. Indicating that he is bothering the class is likely to pressure him into coming in line with his peers.

2. Avoid using sarcastic remarks. Sarcasm is directed toward the person, not the misbehavior. Instead of stopping a minor problem, the teacher may be creating a major problem—direct confrontation with a student.

3. Avoid making threats that are not followed through. Students soon lose respect and confidence in the teacher who states, "Stop that or else!" and the "else" never comes.

4. Avoid inexplicit statements or reprimands like "All right, let's knock it off!" Specify the student, the misbehavior, and the preferred behavior, e.g., "Harold Jones, stop talking to Edward, and finish your math paper."

5. In a tense situation, the use of humor might be the best course of action. Humor has the effect of relaxing students and teacher. Often when a possible challenge is perceived to the teacher's authority, humor can be used to negate the challenge. A teacher who leaves the class laughing somehow puts him/herself in charge of the situation.

   Madge Foster was passing out a class handout that was a little difficult to read because of light print. She apologized by saying, "I know this could be a little darker, but the duplicating machine hasn't been working very well." "That's an understatement," responded one of the students. Madge smiled and quickly replied, "You're right, at my age I'll need a magnifying glass to read it." The students laughed and the class continued.

6. Do not be ashamed or hesitant to ask for help. Many discipline problems have serious emotional backgrounds. Principals, guidance counselors, and school psychologists are there to help teachers—use them.

Schedule Conferences When Necessary. Many teachers wait too long before conducting a student-teacher conference and/or parent-teacher conference to discuss a problem situation. When initial approaches in controlling a student's behavior fail, hold a student-teacher conference. This technique provides the teacher with the opportunity to (1) get to know the student better, (2) identify possible causes of the problem, and (3) plan with the student possible courses of action to solve the problem.

Many parents get extremely upset, as they should, when they find out that their child has been having problems but nothing has been said to them. When initial approaches in controlling a student's behavior fail and the initial student-teacher conference does not seem to work, schedule a parent-teacher conference. Of course, in discipline cases of an extreme nature, an immediate conference with parents might be warranted.

Parents are potentially the teacher's most valuable resource for understanding and dealing with students. They can (1) provide the teacher information necessary for understanding the student's problem, (2) suggest courses of action to be followed in solving the problem, and (3) help both teacher and student in solving the problem.

The following suggestions may be helpful to the teacher when conducting a student-teacher conference:

1. Establish a relaxed atmosphere. If either you or the student are upset, postpone the conference. Little communication will take place if either of you are "about to fly off the handle."

2. Begin the discussion by giving specific examples of the student's strengths, abilities, and acceptable behaviors. Specifics will let the student know that you are observant in the classroom. For example, "Rita, you get along very well with your classmates. Yesterday at recess, I was happy to see you help Janice. Then again today at lunch you were quick to share with Jack."

3. Specify the disruptive behaviors or problems that need attention. Explain to the student why the behavior is disruptive and how it affects the class. Also explain how the behavior affects the student. Allow the student opportunities to explain, discuss, question, etc.

4. Identify courses of action that are open to the student in correcting the problem. Explain how each will help. Make sure he/she understands exactly what is expected and why. If the

course of action selected does not work, he/she should be aware of the next steps you will take. Let the student know you do care and really want to help solve the problem.

5. Summarize the discussion for the student emphasizing the course of action you have both agreed upon.

6. End the conference on a positive note and keep the communication channels open—"John, if you have any problems or are not sure what you are to do, you talk to me."

The following suggestions are provided for teachers conducting a parent-teacher conference:

1. Meet in a setting that is private and, preferably, not over a desk. Move out from behind your desk and sit across from the parents.

2. If the parents are angry or upset, let them blow off steam. When they settle down, begin with *specific examples* of their child's positive attributes. Establish early that you both have a common concern—the welfare of their child.

3. Specify the child's problem, courses of action you have taken, your rationale for selecting the courses of action, and progress made.

4. Ask for suggestions from the parents. Listen and question.

5. Have examples of the child's work and complete records on hand. Although they may not be used, they are readily available if the need arises.

6. Identify and discuss courses of action open to the parents, student, and yourself. Agree upon an approach and determine the necessary steps in solving the problem. Make sure the parents also realize what your next steps will be if this approach fails.

7. Summarize the discussion for the parents. Make sure that they understand what was agreed upon. Also determine how communication concerning their child's progress will be conducted (i.e., by telephone, notes home, another parent conference in two weeks).

8. Leave on a positive note. Many times parents feel a little better if they realize that the problem(s) their child is having may be common and experienced by many other children.

After a student or parent conference, it is a good idea for the teacher to write a summary of what transpired. The summary can be used to refresh the mind in case a subsequent conference is conducted. It can also be useful if the teacher decides to talk to other school personnel—the principal, counselor, or school psychologist—concerning a student's problem.

A second practice worthy of consideration is to talk to the principal, school psychologist, and/or guidance counselor *prior* to conducting a student or parent conference. After becoming familiar with the problem, these school staff members might provide additional suggestions such as ways to relax the participants, other possible courses of action to solve the problem, etc. We feel that such a meeting prior to a conference would be especially beneficial for a beginning teacher.

Finally, a student and/or parent conference can be held at any time. The teacher does not have to wait for a major problem to occur. If a student is perceived to be troubled or a potential problem is seen arising, a conference should be considered. A conference can be a very effective *preventive* technique for minimizing discipline problems.

ORGANIZATIONAL, PLANNING, AND INSTRUCTIONAL PROCEDURES

Physical Environment. Disruptive behaviors can be minimized if the classroom setting is conducive to learning. By manipulating the physical environment, many potential problems can be alleviated. The teacher can ensure that the classroom temperature, ventilation, and lighting are adequate and comfortable for students. Activity areas can be arranged so that clues are provided as to the appropriate behavior for the area. Quiet sections for individual activities such as reading or mathematics should be arranged differently from those that encourage group activities such as block areas. Learning centers can be arranged so that the number of chairs provide a clue as to the number of students who can work in the space at a given time. Materials should be stored near the area where they will be used and should be easily accessible. For example, books used for reference work should be located where students can easily use them without disturbing others.

The encyclopedias in Wanda Wilson's eleventh-grade history class were located on the lower shelf of a bookcase along one side of the room. Whenever a student did research, the fifth-row students nearby had to move as the student crawled to secure the proper volume. After securing the book, the student usually read and took notes on a ventilator. Wanda noticed that minor disturbances occurred anytime someone used the encyclopedias—desks moving, students talking, books and papers falling on the floor. She obtained a table and placed it in the back of the classroom. The table had room for the books and an area for the student to sit, read, and take notes. Using encyclopedias no longer resulted in disturbances.

Peggy Carl is a beginning kindergarten teacher. Prior to the opening of school, she worked for one week preparing her classroom. By the first day of school the room was ready. An aquarium housed tropical fish, a rabbit was a member of the class, the bulletin boards were full of pictures and objects, mobiles hung from the lights, blocks and other materials lined the shelves, and Welcome Clowns were in the corners. Her first two days were a nightmare. The children did not pay attention, they were constantly out of their seats, and during activity periods they bounced from area to area like a ball. In discussing the dilemma with Mrs. Cox, the other kindergarten teacher, it was suggested that many materials and objects be stored for a period of time. The next three days went much more smoothly as students focused more on Ms. Carl, her directions, and the selected activities provided.

Research studies conducted by Kounin (1970) and Brophy and Evertson (1976) identified many specific practices utilized by teachers in minimizing disruptive behaviors. Many of the practices would appear to be applicable to teachers at any grade level. The studies also noted different ways teachers dealt with discipline problems. Successful teachers were identified as those who had a minimum amount of confusion and disruptive behavior in their classrooms. Unsuccessful teachers were identified as those whose classrooms evidenced a great deal of disruption and chaos.

Monitor System. Successful teachers developed a student monitor system to handle routine daily matters such as passing out papers, collecting workbooks, etc. Since students knew exactly what jobs were to be done, when, and by whom, little time was wasted. The unsuccessful teacher's classroom was much more chaotic. Students were not sure what to do, pushing and talking were evident, and a greater amount of time was wasted. Discipline problems were more evident as was the potential for problems to occur.

Al Jacobs is an eighth-grade history teacher. At the beginning of each year, he assigns monitors to help handle emergency exercises such as fire drills and tornado warnings. Students are assigned to open or close windows, turn off lights, lead the group, check roll outside the building, etc. The class practices the drills periodically. When a school alarm is sounded, Mr. Jacobs's classes spend the least amount of time with the fewest disruptions leaving and returning to the classroom.

Helper System. Successful teachers also developed some type of system for students who needed additional help or direction. Some students were designated "helpers" for others who needed additional help with an assignment. Assignments were written and displayed in the classroom to ensure that pupils knew what to do. Times were established for students to secure assistance from the teacher. At other times, the teacher moved around the room and provided individual assistance. In contrast, the unsuccessful teacher was often interrupted by students needing help. Students not knowing what to do next were often frustrated and soon became involved in some type of disruptive behavior.

Sandra Eliot's twelfth-grade sociology classes do a great deal of group work in addition to whole-class assignments. As groups begin a project, Sandra supplies each member with a mimeographed list of requirements, whom to contact in the group if help is needed, and what to do next when a requirement has been finished. In addition, class assignments and instructions for those finishing assignments are listed daily on the chalkboard. Sandra schedules the last fifteen minutes of each class period for assistance to groups or individuals needing her personal help. Periodically she moves about the classroom offering assistance if necessary. Students in her classes understand assignments, know where to go for help, and know what to do next when they finish.

Individual Differences. Successful teachers provided lessons geared to the individual differences of students. When there was a match between the material and student ability and interest, students worked for longer periods of time with fewer interruptions. In addition, successful teachers developed a system so that learners were well aware of what they were to do when they finished an assignment. Specific options were provided for each student, and both teacher and student were aware of acceptable options. In contrast, unsuccessful teachers seemed to have difficulty planning for individual differences. Students in their classes finished their work quickly and then had nothing to do, or could not do the work and gave up. Consequently, disruptive behaviors were likely to occur.

"Withitness". This term, identified by Kounin, refers to the successful teacher's ability to observe events going on in various areas of the classroom. These teachers were able to spot potential problems and redirect student behavior, thus solving the problem before it became a problem. Unsuccessful teachers seemed to become so involved in what they were doing—working with a group, checking papers, etc.—that they failed to recognize potential problems until too late and then had to deal with a disruptive behavior. Students soon become aware that a teacher knows what is going on and are then less likely to try and get away with something.

> Rachael Paul is a second-grade teacher. She makes a point of knowing what each student's assignment is and constantly observes the total class. If children begin to stray, she is quick to direct them back to their assignment. At the beginning of the year, after discussing rules and expectations, she observes children's behavior and is quick to praise students following the rules and meeting expectations. Statements such as "I like the way Robert is placing his work in his folder" provide clues for other children to the behavior she expects. Rachael attempts to ignore minor disruptions during initial class periods. However, as soon as a student is on track, she is quick to reinforce positive behavior. She is very much aware that many children use disruptive behaviors to gain attention. Ignoring the minor disruptions but rewarding positive behavior seems to get many of her students on the right track. Her observations allow for the quick reinforcement of desirable behaviors and time to redirect some behaviors before they become disruptive.

Preclass Work. Faust (1977) and Webster (1968) suggest that junior and secondary high school teachers provide classes with some type of preclass work. This practice encourages students to settle down and puts them in a frame of mind for work. It also provides the teacher time for necessary clerical duties. Students should be held accountable for the work; it should not be just busywork. Webster suggests assignments such as a short quiz or written reaction rather than a reading assignment.

> Bob Carlson is a seventh-grade English teacher, who teaches five sessions of English each day. Bob plans preclass assignments for the beginning five to eight minutes of each class period. Examples of

preclass work include short word puzzles, written reactions to statements and questions, and illustrations of poems and stories that the class has read. Preclass assignments are kept in a notebook by the students and spot-checked periodically by Bob. In addition, students discuss and share some preclass work on Fridays. Often these assignments are related to class assignments but not always. This Thursday the preclass assignment was to write a headline and brief summary describing the results of the recent seventh-grade basketball game.

Variety. Boredom on the part of students usually results in disruptive behaviors. Teachers who use varied approaches in presenting material, unusual or different material geared to student interests, diverse questioning techniques, and who provide students with various ways of responding can help eliminate boredom. It is important for teachers to realize that *they do not* motivate students. All the teacher can do is to provide incentives for students to motivate themselves. Knowledge of student interests and concerns is essential to the teacher who is planning learning activities and experiences that will reduce boredom and actively involve learners.

UNDERSTANDING STUDENT NEEDS AND BEHAVIORS

The goal of helping students develop self-discipline is more likely to be achieved if teachers understand the needs and resultant behaviors of students. Such understanding can provide a greater insight into methods and practices for developing student self-awareness and increased self-discipline.

Student Needs. There are many different human needs and various ways of describing and categorizing them. Gesell and Ilg (1946) were first to provide educators with a comprehensive list of childhood needs, maturational stages, and the educational implications. Since that time, others such as Erikson (1950), Maslow (1954), and Havighurst (1962) have also developed lists of human needs for educators. These lists are important to teachers since they identify the goals students are striving to attain. In addition, lists can be used by teachers as a frame of reference for understanding many student behaviors and providing insight for appropriate learning experiences.

Havighurst's concept of the developmental task provides teachers with a detailed framework for understanding student needs and subsequent behaviors. Havighurst contended that each student progressing toward maturity will encounter at various stages of growth specific developmental tasks based on biological, psychological, and cultural needs. A developmental task

> . . . arises at or about a certain period in the life of the individual, successful achievement of which leads to happiness and to success with later tasks, while failure leads to unhappiness in the individual, disapproval by society, and difficulty with later tasks. (Havighurst 1962, p. 2)

Through an understanding of the developmental tasks, the specific behaviors required at each stage, and successive maturity levels, teachers can gain a clearer picture of the problems of many students. Certainly, an understanding of the problem is the first step in helping a student solve the problem.

Examples of developmental tasks of elementary school children include the following:

1. Achieving increased personal independence
2. Developing positive attitudes about themselves as growing organisms
3. Learning to get along with their peers
4. Developing the necessary academic skills of reading, writing, and mathematics
5. Developing a conscience and a set of basic values.

Some tasks encountered by junior and senior high school students include:

1. Developing increased independence from parents and adults
2. Developing increased social relations with peers
3. Learning to accept themselves as individuals
4. Learning the necessary academic skills and cognitive processes required by society
5. Developing a set of appropriate values and attitudes for directing their behavior.

Teachers who have an understanding of the tasks facing their students can do a great deal to help them achieve these tasks. In other words, elementary and secondary teachers who plan lessons that are interesting and geared to the ability level of a child are not only minimizing the potential for disruptive behavior, but are also helping the student achieve the developmental task of learning the necessary academic skills required by society. The teacher who provides a student the opportunity of self-selection of material and independent work is helping the learner achieve the task of personal independence.

Student Behaviors. As previously mentioned, failure to master a developmental task can lead to unhappiness in the individual and disapproval by society. Thus the accomplishment of tasks is closely related to a student's self-concept and sense of security. Inability to master a task will produce frustration, tension, and anxiety.

> Bobby is a beginning kindergarten student whose parents have been overly protective and quite permissive. Bobby has not been allowed to play with other children because "Some just play too rough." He has always gotten anything he wanted. The few times his parents said no, Bobby has thrown a temper tantrum. This has resulted in getting the no changed to a "Well, O.K."

There is a strong possibility that Bobby will have a difficult time gaining acceptance from his peers and coping with his emotions in a manner acceptable to the school. Bobby may begin to develop frustration, tension, and anxiety toward his kindergarten experiences.

> Karen is a fourth-grade student who is extremely overweight and has protruding front teeth. She is becoming more conscious of her appearance as a result of the mockery and harassment she is beginning to receive from peers. "Fat Karen," "Walrus Karen," and "Hey, Karen, you're ugly" are becoming more common statements during the lunch period and recess. She is the last student to be chosen on a team. When the teacher asks the class to choose a partner, whoever gets Karen complains either verbally or nonverbally.

There can be little doubt that Karen is beginning to find school a frustrating and threatening place. Karen will need help if she is to deal effectively with the situation.

Randy is a tenth-grade student who has become increasingly popular with classmates as a result of his abilities on the basketball team. He is being invited to more parties and asked by more guys to become part of the group. Randy perceives that to be accepted, his hair should be longer, he needs to wear Levi's, and he is going to have to go out more with the group. His parents, however, take pride in his clean-cut appearance and feel one night out a week is enough, and that night has a twelve o'clock curfew.

While to adults, the problem may seem minor and just a part of growing up, to Randy it is of major importance. As he strives for peer acceptance, the difficulties encountered from pressure to conform to parental desires may affect many aspects of Randy's behavior. His academic achievement may begin to decline and/or he may suddenly begin to demonstrate disruptive types of behavior in his classes.

Inability or difficulty in mastering relevant tasks will produce frustration, tension, and anxiety for each student. To cope with the threat, there is strong likelihood that each student may develop or use an *adjustive behavior* to reduce the pressure and anxiety.

Adjustive Behaviors. Perkins (1969) defines an adjustive behavior as a behavior used to reduce frustration, tension, or anxiety. Such behavior is a defense mechanism that everyone uses to some degree to help maintain a stable self-concept. People generally use adjustive behaviors that have been effective in past situations in reducing tensions and anxieties. Perkins identified the following adjustive behaviors: *aggression, repression, substitution, projection, rationalization, withdrawal, fantasy, regression, identification,* and *modifying one's self-concept.* We contend that many of these behaviors are frequently used by students in the school setting. They are often handled as discipline problems and the student is reprimanded. The reasons for and purposes of the behaviors, however, may not be understood by many teachers.

Johnny is a kindergarten student who has been insulated from other adults by his parents. He has also gotten his way at home. He does not like his teacher, Mrs. Jones, telling him what to do. Whenever she directs Johnny to do a certain thing, he scowls at her. Recently he called her a "bitch."

Johnny is using the adjustive behavior referred to as *aggression.* He is trying to remove the source of his frustration, the teacher, through the use of facial expression and abusive language.

Janie is a junior high student who was reprimanded by the teacher of the previous class for not having her work completed. In the next class she directed her frustration to the student teacher saying, "I hate this boring class; your assignments are stupid!"

This form of aggression is called *displacement*. Janie views it unwise to attack the teacher who reprimanded her. So she takes out her frustration on the student teacher whom she views as less powerful.

Sarah told her teacher, mother, and friends that she failed her Spanish test because it was not a fair test. In actuality, Sarah did not study for the test.

Sarah is using the adjustive behavior called *rationalization*. This behavior is used by most people at different times in their lives. Sarah is giving herself and others an acceptable reason in place of the real reason. Certainly if the test were unfair, we would be in sympathy with Sarah.

Allen is a student in Mr. Brown's ninth-grade algebra class who doesn't understand what is going on. When Mr. Brown calls on him, Allen bows his head and says nothing. Soon Mr. Brown calls on another student. Allen doesn't participate in any class discussions and doesn't interact with other students. Mr. Brown feels that Allen is just a shy student.

Allen is using a *withdrawal* behavior to cope with the anxiety perceived in the algebra class. It might be interesting for Mr. Brown to observe Allen's behavior in other situations. He might find out that Allen is not shy at all.

Connie is a very popular sixth-grade student who maintains excellent grades and has been the center of attention. Linda recently enrolled in the class and has also become quite popular. Linda is having a birthday party on Friday afternoon. On Friday morning when Connie heard from friends that they were invited but she was not, she threw a fit—a classic temper tantrum.

Connie is using the adjustive behavior referred to as *regression*. When all else fails, students often revert to behaviors that were successful for them at an earlier age.

The behaviors manifested by Johnny, Janie, and Connie would certainly be viewed as disruptive and would probably be punished. All the behaviors just described, however, are in essence a signal for help. They indicate that students perceive a source of frustration and anxiety and are unable to cope with the situation. These students need help in expressing their emotions and feelings in more appropriate ways.

Teachers who are able to identify adjustive behaviors used by students will be in a better position to help students understand and cope with their emotions. Ignoring or punishing these types of behaviors is not the answer. Forced suppression of feelings may lead students to more detrimental adjustive mechanisms.

Teachers are responsible for helping students understand their own behavior and helping them learn appropriate ways of dealing with frustration and threat. Many educators contend that this goal is as important as the 3 Rs.

Establishing a Conducive Climate. To help students deal with their emotions, the teacher must first establish a classroom climate conducive to student self-expression. This can only be accomplished in a climate that students consider safe for their self-concept. In such a climate, where understanding of self and others is promoted, students will feel accepted as persons of worth and dignity. When they feel that the teacher really cares about them and understands their feelings, when they feel that they will not be ridiculed or laughed at, then students will more readily begin to express their values, concerns, and feelings.

Earlier in this chapter, we presented suggestions for minimizing disruptive behaviors in a classroom situation. We contend that the teacher can establish rules, list expectations, establish control, be firm, and still have a classroom climate that students perceive to be safe for their self-concept. In addition, the teacher can still be viewed by students as a person who cares about them; and if given opportunities, students will express their values, concerns, and feelings. As values and feelings are expressed and discussed, they become more clarified. Once students are able to clarify their values and feelings, they will be in a better position to understand themselves and others. This increases the potential for students to develop more appropriate and satisfying behaviors which can lead to greater degrees of self-discipline and personal growth.

DEVELOPING SELF-DISCIPLINE

We believe that by providing students experiences in dealing with their specific values, attitudes, emotions, and behaviors, the teacher increases the potential for student self-discipline. These areas must be "explored" by each student if she/he is to form an identity and begin to control and direct individual behavior.

Valett (1977, p. 23) contends, and we agree, "that the affective domain of human development has been seriously underrated in education as determined through curriculum offerings and methods of school organization."

Traditional methods for helping students cope with values, attitudes, and emotions have usually included *telling* the students (1) how they should act, (2) how they should feel, (3) what they should desire, and (4) what was right and wrong. These approaches provided little opportunity for students to actively explore the values, attitudes, emotions, and concerns of themselves and others. Many past approaches have emphasized knowing not experiencing—indocrination rather than development through exploration.

Within the past twelve years there has been an increased emphasis on student self-development. A variety of techniques for personal and social development have been recommended in professional texts and journals. Numerous programs have been developed by commercial publishers. Teachers now have at their fingertips a wide assortment of techniques and programs for helping students develop an increased understanding of themselves and others.

There are, however, critics of many of these approaches. Some contend there is no data available to support the effectiveness of many, if any, of the programs. In addition, there is criticism of teaching or dealing with values in school. Some critics maintain there is an invasion of student privacy in some programs, that other approaches allow young and immature students the right to select their own values. Some criticisms may provide teachers with guidelines for the selection and utilization of various techniques. We feel, however, that a majority of the available techniques and programs provide teachers with the necessary suggestions and safeguards for effective utilization.

The following techniques have been used by teachers to help students understand the values, attitudes, emotions, and behaviors of themselves and others. A more detailed list of resources available for teacher use is included in the Appendix.

Dramatic Play. This technique, which is quite popular with elementary teachers, actively involves students in trying out different roles and behaviors. Students with one background or personality style can play the role of another. Shy Bobby becomes Patrick Henry, rich Johnny becomes a poor beggar. Teachers emphasize sincere expression in the various roles so that each student "experiences" the feelings of the characters portrayed. Follow-up discussions can lead students to understand some of their own feelings and the feelings of others.

Role-Playing and Sociodrama. Role-playing is the spontaneous acting out of a situation. Students play the roles of persons and then react or behave as they perceive they should. This technique can provide insight into common individual and group problems. In addition, it provides students the opportunity to test or try out behaviors in a safe study.

> Mr. Clark described John to his ninth-grade class. John never had any trouble getting a date. Whenever a dance was scheduled, John always had a date. Mr. Clark asked for volunteers to play John and call Nancy for a date. At first there was a great deal of giggling. However, after a few students played John and Nancy, you could have heard a pin drop. Mr. Clark was providing students the opportunity to try out an experience that had scared many of the boys to death. The girls were just as interested—how do you say no in a nice manner?

Sociodrama is similar to role-playing in that it is unrehearsed and spontaneous. Sociodrama, however, deals with social problems which are acted out by the group. Shaftel and Shaftel (see Appendix) provide problem stories and excellent guidelines and suggestions for classroom utilization of this technique. We strongly recommend that teachers read this text for ideas pertaining to role-playing and sociodrama as well as dramatic play. While the work is geared to the elementary teacher, many ideas and suggestions could be adapted for grades seven through twelve.

Unfinished and Problem Stories. This technique is appropriate for all grade levels. The approach is similar to role-playing and sociodrama in that personal and group problems are presented. Courses of action and behaviors are not acted out, however; they are discussed by the class under the teacher's guidance. The teacher acts as facilitator and questioner but does not bring personal biases into the discussion. The following actual experience demonstrates the effectiveness of this technique.

Ms. Johnson was a tenth-grade teacher in a large midwestern city. The rock concert, "Jesus Christ Superstar," was coming to the city in three weeks. Ms. Johnson realized that many of her students would be in conflict with their parents concerning attendance at the concert. Some parents would not allow their children to go to "that sacrilege." Ms. Johnson therefore developed an unfinished story related to this student dilemma: *Sally is invited to the concert by a neat guy, then to a party. If she can't go to the concert, no date–no party. Mom and Dad say absolutely no to the concert. Sally does . . .?*

Ms. Johnson's classes discussed the problem, talked about the feelings of Sally, her parents, themselves, and their parents. They listed possible courses of action—consequences for each—and discussed in depth all aspects of the problem.

After the rock group left town, different students thanked Ms. Johnson for helping them by providing "that unfinished story." One student said his parents said absolutely no. However, from the class discussion he had identified a course of action that he would never have thought of—having someone whom the parents really respected approve the concert. His pastor was happy to do so from the pulpit one Sunday before the concert. The pastor had attended the production in New York and recommended that parents as well as teenagers attend. As the student said, "That beats telling them I had to go to the library to study, and then getting caught at the concert."

Questioning Strategies and Self-Analysis Work Sheets. These techniques have become popular through a values clarification approach developed by Simon, Howe, and Kirschenbaum (1972). The purpose of the approach is to help students become aware of and to identify their own values and those of others, and to act according to their value choices. The use of "probing questions" and forced-choice questions is a technique used to help students think through the values they have and why they have them. A second technique, the self-analysis reaction work sheet, has been widely used by many classroom teachers. Here, for example, the student is asked to construct a coat of arms depicting personal achievements, things that make him/her happy, things he/she does well, etc. Another worksheet has the student list twenty things that he/she loves to do. The student then codes the responses according to categories presented by the teacher, such as those items that cost more than three dollars to do, items that his/her parents love doing, etc. While these techniques have been criticized by some, we would encourage teachers to examine the suggested techniques and their theoretical basis.

Bibliotherapy. This technique is used with students on an individual basis. The teacher provides a story about another person having a problem similar to the student's own problem. As a result, students often will view their own problems in a more positive perspective. Resources for developing a better understanding of this technique are included in the Appendix.

CULTURALLY DIFFERENT STUDENTS

Current discussions of discipline usually contain a section pertaining to the disadvantaged or culturally different student and the problem of discipline. As Faust (1977, p.3) noted, "Where the school population is comprised largely of disadvantaged pupils, problems are frequently at a peak."

While we would not disagree with this observation, we do feel that the goals of minimizing disruptive behavior and maximizing student self-discipline can be accomplished with the culturally different student. We believe, however, that the first step toward the accomplishment of these goals is the establishment of a curriculum that accommodates to the unique learning style of each culturally different student.

Castaneda (1972, p. 114) defined this concept as biculturalism where "the child is allowed to freely explore modes of the mainstream culture by means of those preferred modes he brings to school from his home and community." He observed that most educational institutions have an "ideal," Anglo-American middle-class model established which all children are expected to acquire. A child who possesses different modes and who is unable to accommodate to the expected mode will have problems and will certainly encounter anxiety and frustration. We contend that many discipline problems encountered with the culturally different student are related to the student's inability to accommodate to the established mode of the school.

To maximize the development and learning of any child, Castaneda recommended the development of environments prepared to teach children in their preferred modes. Such environments, which he characterized as "culturally democratic," would be cognizant of the fact that students enter school with preferred

46

learning modes, including (1) a language preference, (2) a preferred way of relating to others, (3) an incentive preference, and (4) a preference for thinking, perceiving, remembering, and problem solving.

Without pertinent information on individual students in each of these areas, the teacher's ability to create a culturally democratic environment will be greatly reduced. Castaneda recommended the development of school assessment programs to provide such information.

Learning Styles.* Learning style assessment instruments can provide much of the information suggested by Castaneda. The Dunn and Dunn (1982) instrument, for example, provides information about how children perceive and process information as well as information about conditions that positively affect learning and attitudes toward learning. Carruthers and Young (1980) found that behavior problems were reduced, motivation was increased, and truancy was reduced when time-of-day preferences were matched. Similar results are being discovered in schools across the country as educators become involved in creating learning environments that better match learning styles and brain behavior. Flower Mound Elementary School in Lawton, Oklahoma, has had significant success with a program using brain-compatible learning as defined by Leslie Hart (1983). Kay Johnson (1986), principal of this school, notes that achievement has improved, as has the general attitude of children toward learning. Duffy (1985) suggests that Flower Mound is only one of many schools in Oklahoma who are finding success with teaching techniques designed to match learning styles of children. Readers who wish to explore this area further are encouraged to contact The Learning/Teaching Styles and Brain Behavior Clearinghouse, which is affiliated with the Association for Supervision and Curriculum Development. The Clearinghouse contact person is Jerry Wedlund, Education Building A152, St. Cloud State University, St. Cloud, Minn. 56301.

Contributed by: Dr. Darrell Roubinek, Professor of Elementary Education, and Dr. Hugh Strawn, Assistant Professor of Special Education–Behavior Disorders, Southwest Missouri State University, Springfield, Mo.

CHAPTER 3

Case Studies:
Early Childhood
and Elementary
Education

Chapter 3 includes documented classroom and school-setting incidents and mini-case studies recorded and contributed by classroom practitioners throughout the country. The incidents actually occurred and reflect issues and problems experienced by preschool and elementary teachers and paraprofessionals. The episodes represent a wide spectrum of situations from everyday nuisances and petty actions to critical events.

This collection of real-life encounters involves administrators, teachers, parents, and students. Each incident includes a general description of the background, identification of the specific issue or problem, and a series of questions for discussion, followed by several possible solutions or reactions.

It is advisable that the pre-service or in-service teacher carefully review the mini-case studies and discuss with colleagues the possible solutions and reactions. There is no necessarily best answer or course of action. Recommendations outlined in chapter 2 should be carefully considered when discussing or thinking about a particular incident.

Since the underlying purpose of this collection of incidents is to provoke self-reflection or group discussion, it would also be advisable to carefully review the episodes included in chapter 4 which relate to middle school, junior and senior high school classroom problems.

SELF-CONCERNED PARENT

Background

The cutoff date for nursery school for three-year-olds is September 30; however, the school accepted Michael who wouldn't be three until October 3. The decision to accept him was based on maternal advice—Michael is an only child, has no playmates in the home area, and the mother is expecting an unwanted addition to Michael's world. She feels school has more to offer him than she does at home. Michael proved to be very immature and subject to periods of general disagreement when he sits and does nothing.

Problem

Michael's mother is unable to cope with her son and the problems her pregnancy has created with him. Consequently, she is reaching out for help by sending him to a school situation.

Discussion Questions

1. How can parents help prepare older siblings for a new baby in the family?
2. How could a three-year-old sense his mother's unhappiness with her pregnancy?
3. What other steps could the mother take besides sending her son to school prematurely?
4. How could professional counseling help the mother?

Possible Solutions

1. The school could ask the mother to withdraw Michael because he is too immature.
2. The teacher could isolate Michael when he misbehaves.
3. The teacher could recommend that the mother visit a psychiatrist.
4. The teacher could set up a conference with the mother and attempt to explain that her attitudes and feelings are upsetting her child.

OVERPROTECTIVE PARENT

Background

When four-year-old Kevin and his mother came to register for nursery school, Mrs. Brown stated that Kevin would need plenty of individual love and attention. As the year progressed, she would always call after a morning session and say that Kevin had told her he was picked on in school. Kevin couldn't pinpoint any time or reason, however. His mother complained that he was never hugged or patted. Kevin began to resort to tears that he could easily turn on or off depending on the reaction he wanted. He became very disruptive to gain attention.

Problem

Kevin's mother's apprehension and accusations are beginning to show in Kevin's actions in school. It is apparent that he is testing her as well as his teachers. Her overprotectiveness is encouraging the misbehavior of her son.

Discussion Questions

1. Why might parents believe their child rather than the teacher?
2. Why do some parents find it difficult to let their children take care of themselves in school?
3. How might a teacher give one student attention without neglecting others in the class?

Possible Solutions

1. The teacher could suggest that Kevin and his mother visit a psychiatrist.
2. The teacher could speak with Kevin to determine what seems to be bothering him.
3. The teacher could suggest that Kevin stay home with his mother one more year, because he is too immature for nursery school.

BEHAVIORS FROM HOME

Background

Allen is a four-year-old preschool child. His father is a full-time college student and his mother works full-time. Allen is enrolled in a day-care center for an eight-hour period, five days a week. He is extremely aggressive and cannot keep his hands off the girls. He is constantly pinching, hugging, and trying to kiss them. He has been caught enacting his view of lovemaking with girls on several different occasions.

Problem

Allen's parents feel that love and sex should not be hidden; they are therefore very open about it. Allen has observed his parents' behavior and is trying it out at the day-care center.

Discussion Questions

1. What types of child-rearing practices are prevalent today?
2. What kinds of problems develop when parents model or encourage behaviors that are not generally socially acceptable?
3. How can a teacher accept a child's social or cultural background and still encourage socially acceptable standards?

Possible Solutions

1. The teacher could tell Allen that his behavior is usually not acceptable in public. She could remove him from frequent contact with girls.
2. The teacher could meet with the parents and discuss the problem.
3. The teacher could refer the parents to a counselor or psychologist to discuss the implications of Allen's behavior for his development.
4. The teacher could inform the parents that since she is also responsible for other children, Allen will be dismissed from the program if this behavior continues.

THE AGGRESSIVE CHILD

Background

Benny is a five-year-old kindergarten student of above-average ability who is usually an excellent student. However, he is very aggressive with his peers. He shoves, talks loudly, and even strikes if he doesn't get his way. This behavior is very prevalent before school, at recess, and after school. Benny doesn't act aggressively with his teacher or at home, however.

Problem

Benny's father is a police officer. Benny feels that aggressive behavior is necessary to get his way.

Discussion Questions

1. What are reasons for some children's overaggressive behavior?
2. In what ways do parents and teachers "teach" or reinforce aggressiveness?
3. Should some types of aggressive behavior be encouraged?

Possible Solutions

1. The teacher could have a conference with the parents and discuss a possible solution.
2. Benny's father could be invited to the class to talk about "How Police Officers Help People."
3. The teacher could talk to Benny about his behavior to help him understand he doesn't always have to be first.
4. The teacher could praise Benny whenever he works cooperatively with his peers.

A STUDENT WITHDRAWS

Background
Becky is a five-year-old kindergarten student who is very intelligent, responsive, and active. After the school year began, the teacher noticed that Becky has a slight stutter and her speech isn't always clear. Becky tried to speak in class until classmates laughed and made fun of her.

Problem
Becky has withdrawn and refuses to speak in class.

Discussion Questions
1. When the teacher noticed that Becky had a speech problem, should he have had her try to speak in front of the class?
2. How can young children be helped to accept differences in other children?
3. Why do some parents not inform teachers of problems their children have?

Possible Solutions
1. The teacher could meet with Becky and help build her confidence.
2. The teacher could refer Becky to a speech therapist.
3. The teacher could talk to the class about how it feels to be laughed at.
4. The teacher could meet with Becky's parents and the speech therapist to discuss ways they could help Becky.
5. The teacher could arrange that Becky does not have to talk in front of the class until she becomes more confident.

CHILD REFUSES TO ACKNOWLEDGE MISTAKES

Background
Jeff is a first-grade boy who is very bright and a joy to have in a classroom. He is extremely popular with other students. If corrected for anything, however, Jeff refuses to accept that he has made a mistake or broken a rule. He responds, "I didn't do it." Subsequent discussions with his mother revealed that "This has been his way of life. We've tried to change him, but it's impossible."

Problem
Jeff has a problem that his parents seem to be aware of. They are more or less resigned that this is the way he is going to be.

Discussion Questions
1. Why would Jeff use this behavior in the classroom?
2. How can schools help parents better understand and cope with the behavior of their children?
3. Why do parents often just accept certain behaviors of their children?

Possible Solutions

1. The teacher could punish Jeff for this type of behavior.
2. The teacher could meet with Jeff and discuss other ways of behaving when he is corrected.
3. The teacher could meet with the parents to discuss a course of action both would follow in helping Jeff learn more appropriate behaviors.
4. The parents could be referred to a counselor or psychologist for help in changing Jeff's behavior.

MS. EXAGGERATION

Background

Irene is a most capable first-grade student. She comes from a middle-class family and has parents who are very concerned about her success in school. Irene causes few problems in the class other than her "storytelling." She makes up fantastic lies about family vacations, toys she owns, people her family knows, etc. Recently, when other students called her a liar, Irene burst into tears and sobs of "I am not." Her stories have continued, however.

Problem

Irene's behavior is becoming increasingly more disruptive to the class. Why is she exaggerating so?

Discussion Questions

1. Why do children exaggerate the truth?
2. How might parents interpret their child's exaggerations in school?
3. Is exaggeration a normal behavior for a child?
4. What are some ways that a teacher can discuss this behavior with a child without calling the student a liar?

Possible Solutions

1. The teacher could meet with the parents to discuss Irene's behavior. Does she demonstrate this behavior at home?
2. The teacher could begin giving Irene attention and praise for acceptable behavior.
3. The teacher could talk to Irene about her stories and how other students feel about them, jealousy, etc. She could encourage Irene just to tell "little things" that her classmates will understand.
4. Irene could be referred to a counselor or school psychologist.

MR. FANTASY

Background

David is a six-year-old first grader who lives with his mother and grandmother in a rural community. He is small for his age and stays to himself. He seldom completes his work; instead, he spends most of his time gazing out the window. He seems to daydream most of the time. Subsequently, he never knows what is going on in the class.

Problem

David is a daydreamer.

Discussion Questions

1. Why do students daydream or live in a fantasy world?
2. Why might students who daydream in class not be daydreamers at home?
3. What are some other behavior labels given to students who daydream in class?

Possible Solutions

1. The teacher could meet with the parents to discuss David's problem. Is David a daydreamer at home?
2. The teacher could engage David in activities that ensure his success and be quick to praise him.
3. The teacher could refer David for a hearing test.
4. The teacher could meet with David to make sure he understands what is expected of him and to determine how he feels in class.
5. The teacher could punish David for not paying attention and completing his work and praise him when he does.

MS. I'M-SO-DIFFERENT-FROM-MY-SISTER

Background

Barbara is an eight-year-old second grader who comes from a fine family. She has a younger brother and an older brother and sister. Her older brother and sister were "model" students whose behavior and grades were excellent. Barbara is another story. While she has the ability, she does not use it. Her work is sloppy and usually not completed. She constantly talks, is out of her seat, and in any other way will disrupt the class. A conference with her parents revealed that Barbara is also their "problem" child.

Problem

Barbara is striving to be herself by not following the examples of older siblings who were "model" students.

Discussion Questions
1. Why are siblings often so different?
2. How do parents and teachers foster sibling rivalry?
3. What can parents do to decrease competition among siblings?
4. What safeguards can a teacher take to decrease competition?

Possible Solutions
1. The teacher could talk to Barbara and encourage her to be herself.
2. The teacher could meet with the parents to discuss ways that Barbara might be helped in finding her own life-style.
3. The teacher could use the interests that Barbara has as an incentive for achievement and desirable behavior.
4. The teacher could identify Barbara's interests and encourage her to share them with the class.

PARENT HOSTILE TO CHILD

Background

Cheryl is an illegitimate eight-year-old second grader with an average IQ. Previously she attended a behavior disorders special class because of stealing food, money, and belongings of classmates. She lives with her mother and two illegitimate half brothers, and appears to be physically abused and inadequately fed. Her mother hates Cheryl's father for deserting them and takes her revenge on Cheryl. When her mother punishes her for any achievement, Cheryl reacts by urinating or defecating on her mother's bed. Cheryl has had many psychological tests.

Problem

Cheryl appears to be physically abused. She constantly lies and steals and has no friends.

Discussion Questions
1. Why do parents abuse their children?
2. To whom should a teacher report a suspected child abuse or neglect case?
3. Is a teacher protected by law for reporting a child abuse case?
4. Is a teacher required by law to report a suspected abuse case?

Possible Solutions
1. The teacher could notify the human resources department about the family situation.
2. The teacher could call the juvenile judge and report the case.
3. The teacher could call the local police department and report the case.
4. The teacher *should* make the classroom atmosphere as safe and secure as possible for Cheryl.

PARENTS CAN'T ACCEPT CHILD'S PROBLEM

Background

Brian is an eight-year-old second grader. He is a well-behaved boy who is well liked by his peers. Brian has great difficulty with his reading because of an IQ just above the special education level. His mother will not give her permission to put him in the special education class. She is more concerned with keeping him out of that class. Brian's stepfather doesn't want to get involved at all. Brian can hardly wait for summer to come so he won't have to read anymore.

Problem

Brian's best interests are being sacrificed because of the stigma of special education.

Discussion Questions

1. How can mainstreaming a child help erase the stigma of being in a special education class?
2. What other resources are available to parents for helping a student with a reading problem?
3. Should the school put the child in a special education class even if the parents oppose the idea?

Possible Solutions

1. The guidance counselor could invite the parents to school to observe a special education class.
2. The teacher could keep trying to convince the parents that they would be helping Brian by letting him participate in a special education class.
3. A tutor could be obtained so that Brian might have special aid.
4. The teacher could recommend a special reading program for Brian in the summer so that he might catch up with his classmates in reading.

UNCONCERNED PARENT

Background

Karen is the youngest in a family of three girls. Her sisters are fifteen and seventeen. Karen is currently repeating second grade. She lives at home with her sisters and father since her mother's death; however, she spends most of her time with an aunt and uncle. Her retention in second grade was based on her reading and emotional problems. Karen is very aggressive, and her play activities center around football and softball. She has a poor attitude toward school.

Problem

Karen's father seems unconcerned with her problems at school.

Discussion Questions

1. Why might Karen's interest center on football and softball?
2. What are your feelings about retaining a student?
3. How might Karen's sisters help with the problem?
4. Why might a parent who loves his child seem unconcerned about her school work?
5. What can schools do about teaching the concept of death?

Possible Solutions

1. The teacher could suggest that the school counselor meet with the parent, aunt and uncle, and sisters to discuss Karen's problem.
2. The teacher could involve Karen in class activities, giving her more responsibility and praise.
3. Karen could be referred to the school counselor or school psychologist for help with her emotional problems.
4. Football and softball could be used as an incentive for Karen to work harder in reading.

PARENTS REFUSE TO ACCEPT PROBLEM

Background

Betty is a nine-year-old second grader. Her mother deserted the family seven years ago leaving the father to raise Betty, a twelve-year-old brother, and a seventeen-year-old sister. The father is a truck driver who has frequent women visitors. Betty has had to sleep on the floor so that a "visitor" could have her bed. She is usually poorly groomed and not accepted by her peers. Betty is the lowest student in her class academically; she fantasizes a great deal whenever a classmate will listen.

Problem

Her father is unwilling to accept that Betty's social and academic problems stem from her home life.

Discussion Questions

1. Should school personnel interfere in the private lives of students? If so, under what circumstances?
2. What community agencies might be notified about a situation of this kind?
3. How can teachers best help children from bad home situations?

Possible Solutions

1. The teacher could report the problem to the human resources department and let them handle it.
2. The teacher could set up a conference with the father to explain how his life-style is detrimental to his children.
3. The teacher could give as much special care and attention to Betty as humanly possible. The classroom setting should be safe and secure for Betty.

MS. TATTLETALE

Background

Ellen is a very sweet third-grade student. She does excellent work and has parents who are very concerned about her achievement and conduct. However, Ellen drives the teacher crazy.

Problem

Ellen is a constant tattletale. She must have eyes in the back of her head. Nothing goes on in the class that she doesn't know about. When an incident is unacceptable, Ellen reports the person and action quickly and loudly.

Discussion Questions

1. What are some reasons that children tattle?
2. How do parents and teachers encourage tattling?
3. How can teachers help students understand the difference between tattling and telling something they should tell?
4. Why is tattling and telling less prevalent at the junior and senior high level?

Possible Solutions

1. The teacher could talk to Ellen about her tattling and how the problem might be solved. Ellen could be rewarded when she doesn't tattle and ignored or punished when she does.
2. The teacher could discuss Ellen's problem with her parents for a possible solution.
3. The teacher could refer Ellen to a counselor or psychologist for special help.
4. The teacher could establish "tattling and telling" rules for the class to follow.

PARENTAL EXPECTATIONS

Background

Shawna is in third grade. She is nine years old, very pretty, extremely conscientious, and works very hard on any assignments. Shawna is an overachiever. On recent group achievement tests Shawna's scores were average. Her parents were outraged and insisted that she be tested again. Subsequent tests revealed the same results. The parents began putting pressure on Shawna to work harder.

Problem

Her parents cannot accept Shawna's achievement abilities.

Discussion Questions

1. What is "overachievement"?
2. What are some ways that a teacher can identify an overachiever?
3. Why is it harmful for the overachiever not to be identified early?
4. How might the concept of overachievement be explained to parents?

Possible Solutions

1. The teacher could meet with the parents to discuss the harmful effects of the pressure being exerted on Shawna.
2. The teacher could refer the parents to a child psychologist.
3. If Shawna doesn't seem to be bothered by the pressure, the teacher could ignore it.

PARENTS HOSTILE TO EACH OTHER

Background

Joan is a very likable, above-average, nine-year-old third grader who has three older sisters and a six-year-old brother. Her father is a professional, and her mother was recently discharged from an alcoholic rehabilitation center. All the children except Joan have accepted the home situation. Their father, who prefers to live in his own apartment, is more liked by his children than their mother. Joan loves both her parents and her siblings. Her schoolwork doesn't compare favorably with her past record. She misses school frequently, and when she is in school often has imaginary pains and illnesses. A physical examination indicated she is in good health.

Problem

Joan loves both her parents, has become emotionally insecure, is an underachiever in school, and is becoming psychosomatic.

Discussion Questions

1. How can elementary school counselors play an important role in the lives of their students?
2. What should a teacher do who knows that professional help is needed by a student?
3. How might a child's behavior in school be an indication that something is wrong at home?

Possible Solutions

1. The teacher could ask the school guidance counselor to call a meeting with both parents to talk over Joan's behavior and its implications.
2. The teacher could call Joan's father, talk with him, and suggest that he and his wife talk with Joan and explain they both love her but have problems that force them to live the way they have been living.
3. The teacher could talk to Joan and try to explain that parents may often have marital problems but still love their children very much.

A STUDENT'S SOURCE OF MONEY

Background

Ethel is a nine-year-old fourth grader, an above-average student who has always been most cooperative in class. She is from a poverty-level family and is on a free lunch program. Recently, Ethel has been involved in a series of commotions after lunch. She is buying candy from classmates during class period.

Problem

Ethel, with no apparent source of funds, buys candy from classmates after lunch. Where is she getting the money?

Discussion Questions

1. Where could Ethel be getting the money?
2. Should a teacher ignore this situation?
3. What might be the reaction of other parents if they found out Ethel was buying candy from their children?

Possible Solutions

1. The teacher could ignore the candy buying and tell Ethel to buy it when she won't disturb the class.
2. The teacher could talk to Ethel about the source of the money.
3. The teacher could talk with the parents about the source of the money.
4. The teacher could inform the principal and let her handle the situation.

MR. QUICK-FINGERS

Background

Billy is a nine-year-old fourth-grade student from a middle-class family. He is adopted and the only child in the family. Billy's parents will give him just about anything he wants and will do anything for him.

Problem

Billy steals anything in sight. He takes pencils, books, and personal belongings of other children.

Discussion Questions

1. What are some reasons that students steal?
2. What can be done for students who see their parents steal?
3. What can a teacher do to minimize stealing in the classroom?

Possible Solutions

1. The teacher could talk with Billy and try to agree on a way to work out his problem.
2. The teacher could make a deal. If Billy doesn't steal, he will be given some things that he likes, such as team captain, extra time to work on a model plane, etc.
3. The teacher could arrange a conference with the parents, teacher, and counselor to help share the problem.
4. The teacher could refer Billy to a counselor or psychologist for special help.

PARENTS IN CONFLICT WITH REAL MOTHER

Background

Jerry is a bright fourth-grade student who does excellent work and tries his best daily. He lives with his father and stepmother. His real mother, who lives in a nearby town, wants to be a part of his life. She has been to school to inquire about Jerry and has observed him in the classroom. Jerry seems thrilled that she is interested in his schoolwork. His father and stepmother do not know that the real mother has been at school. During a recent conference with the father and stepmother, the teacher found out that they do not want Jerry's real mother to have any contact with him unless it has been prearranged with them.

Problem

Jerry is in the middle of a family situation that might be detrimental to him. The teacher is also caught in the middle.

Discussion Questions

1. Does the teacher have a responsibility to adhere to the desire of the father and stepmother?
2. Should the teacher tell the parents that the real mother has already visited Jerry?
3. What are some possible problems for Jerry that can arise from the situation?

Possible Solutions

1. The teacher could discuss the problem and a possible course of action with the real mother.
2. The teacher could refer the parents to the principal, since all visitors must be cleared at that point.
3. The teacher could ask the principal to check into the legal implications of the situation.
4. The teacher could tell the parents that without a court order the real mother could not be kept from visiting her child.
5. The teacher could meet with the parents, counselor, and principal to discuss the situation and the problems it might pose for Jerry.

A NEW STUDENT

Background
Maria is a nine-year-old fifth-grade student of above-average intelligence who recently transferred from a school in another state. From day one Maria has had problems adjusting. She does not keep her mind on her work, leaves much of her work unfinished, and is constantly out of her seat talking to other students. When corrected she retorts, "I know," "I was going to finish it," "I didn't understand the assignment," or "I am just finding out what to do next."

Problem
Maria is having difficulty adjusting to her new class and seems to be rationalizing her behavior.

Discussion Questions
1. What kinds of anxieties do students have when transferring to a new school?
2. What can teachers do specifically to help a new student adjust?
3. What kind of family problems might cause a move? How might these problems affect a child?

Possible Solutions
1. The teacher could talk to Maria and explain class rules and teacher expectations.
2. The teacher could assign Maria a "welcome partner(s)" to help her learn her way around. The partner(s) would be a "model" student(s).
3. The teacher could praise Maria for acceptable behaviors and completion of assignments.
4. The teacher could meet with the parents to discuss any other problems Maria might be having, such as coping with recently divorced parents, etc.

A STUDENT BUYS FRIENDS

Background
Dale is a clever ten-year-old fifth-grade boy. He is very bright but hasn't been very popular with other students. During a math period a great deal of note-passing was observed by the teacher who also found out that Dale has been taking "orders" from other students of what they would like and then buying the things for them. Dale is from a very wealthy family.

Problem
Dale feels rejected by his peers and is trying to buy their friendship.

Discussion Questions

1. What are different ways that students try to win friends?
2. Why might Dale use money rather than some other technique?
3. In what ways do teachers make a student popular or unpopular?

Possible Solutions

1. The teacher could meet with Dale and suggest another course of action for peer acceptance.
2. The teacher could meet with Dale's parents to discuss the problem.
3. The teacher could ignore the situation and help Dale learn a more acceptable way of achieving peer acceptance.
4. The teacher could punish Dale for disrupting the class and tell the class he wants the order-taking stopped.

UPSET PARENTS

Background

Robert is an eleven-year-old fifth-grade student of average ability. Notes were sent home during the first grading period indicating that he was not completing his assignments. Only a few of the notes were received by Robert's parents. After grades were assigned, the parents arrived at school quite hostile and angry. They contended that the problem is a personality clash between Robert and the teacher.

Problem

While Robert was having problems, there was a definite communication problem between the teacher and parents.

Discussion Questions

1. What are some problems associated with sending notes home with students?
2. What are some effective techniques for communicating with parents?
3. Where could the parents get the idea there is a personality clash between Robert and the teacher?

Possible Solutions

1. The principal could reassign Robert to another teacher with a specific recommendation: communicate promptly and effectively.
2. The teacher could meet with the parents to work out an acceptable solution.
3. The principal could meet with the teacher, parents, and Robert to clarify the problem and seek an acceptable solution.

A TOO-BUSY STUDENT

Background

Kelly is a twelve-year-old sixth-grade student who has been diagnosed as learning disabled. He is the youngest of four children whose parents are in their late fifties. The family needs extra money and Kelly contributes by having a paper route. In addition, his parents have arranged a before-school job at a local cafe. The boy is disinterested in schoolwork and always seems tired from his jobs.

Problem

His parents feel that since Kelly is "handicapped," he should start working as soon as possible. The family also needs the money.

Discussion Questions

1. What are the various educational labels given to different kinds of handicapping conditions?
2. What can schools do to make all parents more aware of the nature of various handicaps?
3. What are some rewarding and lucrative occupations that employ various handicapped persons?

Possible Solutions

1. The teacher and counselor could meet with the parents and explain Kelly's potential for achievement and school success.
2. The teacher could suggest to the principal that Kelly be allowed to sleep during recess, physical education, and other nonacademic areas. In that way he would be fresh for academic subjects.
3. The teacher could suggest enrolling Kelly in a work-study program, where he could earn money and achieve educationally at the same time.

AN "OVERDEVELOPED" STUDENT

Background

Trudy is a well-developed sixth-grade girl who has been absent from school the first five Thursdays of the year. She has brought notes from her mother each Friday explaining that Trudy was ill. Trudy spends a great deal of time primping and reading romantic magazines. She never becomes involved in games at recess. Thursday is P.E. day, and the P.E. instructor is a young, good-looking, male teacher.

Problem

Trudy seems to be maturing faster than her peers and is self-conscious about her physical development.

Discussion Questions

1. How can teachers help students accept their physical differences and the differences of others?
2. What are some physical differences that are likely to lead to self-consciousness or ridicule by other students?
3. Should a teacher have a conference with parents of a child who is "physically different" concerning potential problems immediately, or wait to see if a problem materializes?

Possible Solutions

1. The teacher could talk to Trudy and help her accept the fact that while she is different she should not be ashamed.
2. The teacher could meet with the parents and discuss the problem.
3. Trudy could be excused from P.E. until she can handle the situation.
4. Special provisions could be made during P.E. so that Trudy would not have to be embarrassed.

IS STUDENT TELLING THE TRUTH?

Background

Donna is a very intelligent twelve-year-old sixth grader. She is an excellent student who does a superior job on any project she turns in. Recently when a social studies booklet was due, Donna claimed she had already turned hers in, that it must have been misplaced. Later that day when the teacher spoke on the phone with Donna's mother concerning a class party, the conversation revealed that Donna had left her social studies booklet at home. When the teacher mentioned this to Donna, she insisted she had done *two* identical booklets.

Problem

Donna seems to be telling a lie.

Discussion Questions

1. Give some reasons for students lying and cheating in school.
2. React to this statement: Many teachers make liars and cheaters out of students.
3. What can a teacher do to minimize lying and cheating?
4. What would be the pros and cons of the teacher's accepting Donna's explanation.

Possible Solutions

1. The teacher could tell Donna that he didn't believe her and lower her grade on the social studies booklet.
2. The teacher could meet with Donna and discuss the problem in an attempt to get at the cause of her behavior.
3. The teacher could meet with Donna's parents and discuss the problem.
4. The teacher could accept the booklet and say nothing more.

STUDENT LIES TO PARENTS

Background

Cindy is a very mature twelve-year-old sixth-grade student. She is very intelligent and good grades come easily to her. She is the youngest child in the family and is still referred to as the baby. If Cindy does not get her way at school, she sulks and has been known to blurt out obscenities. Her parents are very religious and would not condone such behavior. They feel that some mistake must have been made, since Cindy told them she hasn't done anything wrong.

Problem

Her parents refuse to believe that Cindy is wrong, since she is able to convince them she is right.

Discussion Questions

1. Why do students sometimes develop attitudes and behaviors quite different from those of their family?
2. Why is it difficult for parents to accept the fact that their children have problems and make mistakes?
3. What other persons might have first-hand knowledge of Cindy's unacceptable behavior?

Possible Solutions

1. The teacher could talk with Cindy and let her know that sooner or later her parents will learn the truth.
2. The teacher could document specifics and have other students, Cindy's scout leader, a teacher-aide, etc., do the same. The teacher could then meet with the parents and present these findings.
3. Cindy could be referred to the school counselor or psychologist for special help.

MR. I-HATE-THE-WORLD

Background

Eliot is a seventh-grade student who walks around with a chip on his shoulder. He is of below-average ability academically and has been retained twice in his school career. While his parents seem concerned, they feel that Eliot will be like his father—"School's not his thing." Eliot has few friends and doesn't seem to care. In fact, he just sits in class and does nothing and is extremely antisocial toward peers and teachers.

Problem

Eliot's self-concept in relation to school is very low. He feels he never really had a chance and has little use for teachers or students who achieve or try to achieve.

Discussion Questions

1. What type of special programs do schools need for students like Eliot?
2. What other types of behaviors are demonstrated by students "with a chip on their shoulders"?
3. What can teachers do to help improve the self-concept of junior-high-school-aged students?

Possible Solutions

1. The teacher could send Eliot to the counselor for special help.
2. The teacher could ignore Eliot since his behavior is not disruptive.
3. The teacher could meet with the parents and counselor to discuss a possible solution.
4. Eliot could be enrolled in a work-study program.

TOO SMART FOR THE TEACHER

Background

Ted is an extremely intelligent seventh grader with an IQ score on record of 146. Ted began the school year in a very positive manner. In English class he quickly finished all assignments and was given extra assignments by the teacher to keep him busy. Recently Ted has slowed down considerably, has started talking to other students and causing disruptions. When the teacher questioned him about his behavior, he retorted, "When I finish, you just give me more busywork; I'll just do what the rest of the class does."

Problem

Ted is a gifted student who is not challenged by the classroom work, and he is becoming bored.

Discussion Questions

1. What provisions can schools make for gifted students?
2. How would you define a gifted student?
3. What kinds of problems are encountered by gifted students in school?
4. How do some students react or adjust to these problems?

Possible Solutions

1. The teacher could apologize to Ted and work out individual assignments based on his interests and abilities.
2. The teacher could meet with the principal and discuss Ted's placement in advanced classes for certain periods of instruction.
3. The teacher could require Ted to do the work assigned the rest of the class or be punished.
4. The teacher could recommend to the parents that Ted be enrolled in a school with a gifted program.

MS. SOCIETY

Background

Robin is a very popular eighth-grade student. She is an honor student and is encouraged by her parents to become involved in all school activities. In addition, Robin is very active in social groups outside school. Recently, her assignments have been turned in late and are of poor quality. Robin apologized for the quality of the work and stated she has been just too busy. She also commented that her mother feels "it's not as important what you know as whom you know."

Problem

Her parents' encouragement and pressure to make Robin "Ms. Society" are distracting her from achievement.

Discussion Questions

1. What types of activities are students encouraged to join by their parents?
2. Why do some parents pressure their children to become involved in these activities?
3. What kinds of pressures do these activities create for students?

Possible Solutions

1. The teacher could inform Robin that she will either do the work she is capable of or receive a lower grade.
2. The teacher could meet with the parents and discuss the problem that Robin is having.
3. The teacher could give Robin less work since it is evident that she is capable.

THE CLASS CLOWN

Background

Walter is an eighth-grade student who loves being the class clown. His work is below average and he comes from a home that doesn't value education. He loves making wisecracks and listening to his friends laugh. He is popular since he has a motorcycle and calls himself the "Fonz." Grades, staying after school, parent conferences, and even being expelled do not phase him in the least.

Problem

Walter finds school a bore and loves to be the center of attention.

Discussion Questions

1. What are some common concerns and interests of junior high students?
2. What kinds of incentives can teachers offer junior high students who find school boring?
3. How can a teacher "stay current" with the interests and concerns of students?
4. What can schools do to gain the support of parents who have themselves had an unhappy school experience?

Possible Solutions

1. The teacher could meet with Walter and find out what really interests him. If possible, class discussions could be planned in this area. If Walter wisecracked, he would be sent out of the class.
2. The teacher could send Walter to a counselor for special help.
3. Ex-students who had an attitude similar to Walter's but who "saw the light" could be brought in to talk about their experiences.
4. Walter could be sent to the principal, counselor, or study hall to complete his lessons thus denying him interaction with peers.
5. Class discussions that interested the class could be planned. Since Walter's wisecracks would distract from the discussion, his peers would force him into line.

VIEWPOINT

YOU CAN'T REMEDIATE THE CAUSE

As I work with preservice and inservice teachers, I often hear them say, "What can I do? His home environment is terrible, his parents don't even care." Engelmann (1969, p. 9) contends that a teacher "...must limit her attention to specific skills the child has and doesn't have, because she can work only on the child's performance not on his history or his home." Other authorities feel that the value of knowing the cause lies in helping teachers to more fully understand the problem.

Your Viewpoint: How important is information related to the cause of a student's problem? Will too much adverse information cause the teacher to give up, to quit trying?

Contributed by Dr. Hugh Strawn, Assistant Professor of Special Education–Behavior Disorders, Southwest Missouri State University, Springfield, Mo.

CHAPTER 4

Case Studies: Middle School, Junior and Senior High School

Like the preceding chapter, chapter 4 includes documented classroom and school-setting incidents and mini-case studies recorded and contributed by classroom practitioners throughout the country. The incidents presented here actually occurred and reflect issues and confrontations experienced by middle school, junior and senior high school teachers. These episodes represent a wide spectrum of situations from everyday nuisances to critical events and involve administrators, teachers, student teachers, students, parents, and guardians.

As in chapter 3, each incident includes a general classification, background statement, identification of the specific issue or problem, and a series of questions for discussion, followed by several possible solutions or reactions. Disciplinary incidents are common to teachers in all subjects; the incidents included in this chapter therefore represent happenings in many academic disciplines and fields of study common to most secondary school curricula.

Here, too, it is advisable that the pre-service or in-service teacher carefully review the mini-case studies and discuss possible solutions and reactions with colleagues. There is no necessarily best answer or course of action. Recommendations outlined in chapter 2 should also be carefully considered when discussing or thinking about a particular episode.

Classroom incidents involving elementary and secondary teachers are not necessarily mutually exclusive. It is therefore suggested that secondary teachers carefully review the mini-case studies outlined in chapter 3 and that elementary educators review those in chapter 4.

PARENT INTERVENES IN CHILD'S SOCIAL LIFE

Background

Roy and Amy are juniors who have been going steady for almost a year. Roy's mother does not want her son to get serious with any particular girl because she has big plans for him in the future. When his mother found out that Roy and Amy sit next to each other in one of their classes, she became upset. She called the teacher and asked that the two be separated so that they will have as little contact as possible during the class.

Problem

A parent who wishes to manage her son's social life asks the teacher to intervene.

Discussion Questions

1. If Roy finds out about his mother's request of the teacher, what do you suppose his reaction might be?
2. Should a parent ask a teacher to intervene in his or her child's social life?
3. How might the teacher separate the two young people without causing hard feelings?
4. Does the teacher have a greater responsibility to the parent or to the student?

Possible Solutions

1. The teacher can do as the parent suggests.
2. The teacher can refuse to do as the parent suggests.
3. The teacher can tell the students what Roy's mother requested and ask them to separate.
4. The teacher can tell the parent that the two young people have caused no problem in the class and that he would rather not disturb matters by moving them.

STUDENT HOOKED ON DRUGS

Background

Larry, a sophomore from a broken home, has recently begun taking drugs. His friends are extremely concerned and have tried to talk some sense into him. Larry, who has a flair for dramatics, enjoys being the center of attention and feels this is one way to gain even more attention. His friends spoke with Larry's homeroom teacher to see if she had any suggestions.

Problem

A young man begins popping pills as a way of gaining his friends' attention. His behavior in class becomes noticeably different and his friends and the teacher become concerned.

Discussion Questions

1. What are some reasons that today's teenagers turn to drugs?
2. How can peers help students get away from the drug scene?
3. What should teachers do when they realize a student is on drugs?
4. How do classroom experiences contribute toward driving a student to drugs or keeping him/her away from them?

Possible Solutions

1. The teacher should talk to Larry and point out the dangers of drug abuse.
2. The teacher should explain to Larry the concern his friends have.
3. The teacher should call Larry's guardian and report what she knows and has observed.
4. The teacher should turn Larry in to the principal for disciplinary action.

STUDENTS RESENT NEW TEACHER

Background

A new teacher, Ms. Rios, is sponsor of the student newspaper. Several members of the previous year's staff seem to resent the new teacher and constantly refer to the way things used to be run. Ms. Rios realizes that her style of teaching is different from that of the previous teacher, but she tries to overlook critical comments made by some students. One day, however, she reached the breaking point when the editor ran down the hall to get advice from the former sponsor rather than checking with her first.

Problem

A new teacher finds it difficult to replace another well-liked, experienced teacher.

Discussion Questions

1. How should new teachers deal with students who seem to resent them?
2. Just how long can teachers ignore unkind criticism about themselves?
3. How can experienced teachers help new teachers get through their first year more easily?
4. Should new teachers expect to have more discipline problems than older teachers? Why or why not?

Possible Solutions

1. The new teacher should talk with the students who seem most resentful and try to understand them better.
2. The new teacher should ask the experienced teacher to speak to the students about their unkind remarks and attitude of resentment.
3. The teacher should try to ignore the remarks and try to gain the students' loyalty with time and patience.
4. The teacher should dismiss the students from the activity because of their rudeness.

STUDENT TOO AFFECTIONATE WITH TEACHER

Background

A middle-aged teacher is worried about the exuberant affection a junior boy shows toward her. He occasionally puts his arm around her or slaps her on the back when he sees her. The student comes from a large family where much affection is shown, so the teacher feels hesitant about telling the boy how she feels.

Problem

A teacher feels troubled by displays of affection shown her by a student of the opposite sex.

Discussion Questions

1. Is it all right for teachers to hug or show other signs of affection toward high school students?
2. How could frequent physical contact between students and teachers cause problems?
3. How can a teacher let a student know tactfully that he or she does not like a certain type of behavior?
4. How do people use nonverbal communication to let others know how they feel?

Possible Solutions

1. The teacher can ask the boy to keep his hands off her and explain why she feels the way she does.
2. The teacher can try to evade the student when she sees him approaching.
3. The teacher can explain that she feels uncomfortable about his hugging her, particularly in front of other people.
4. The teacher should ignore what the student does and be thankful there are affectionate students around.
5. The teacher should hug the student if he hugs her.

PARENT ASKS TEACHER TO COUNSEL SON

Background

Mrs. Williams came to school one afternoon to speak with her 17-year-old son's French teacher. She was very distraught because her son has been dating a 29-year-old divorcée. Her son has been offered a scholarship to a prestigious university, but the mother is worried that he is being led astray and will not continue his education. The mother begged the teacher to talk to her son.

Problem

A parent seeks help from her son's favorite teacher. The parent hopes the teacher can talk some sense into her son's head.

Discussion Questions

1. Does the teacher have the right to meddle in a student's "affairs"?
2. Will the mother's attitude toward her son help the situation or hurt it? Why?
3. If the teacher does speak to the student, what should she say?

Possible Solutions

1. The teacher can advise the mother to avoid making an issue of the situation, as the romance will probably die out on its own eventually.
2. The teacher can speak with the young man and try to help him avoid making a serious mistake.
3. The teacher can tell the student that his mother is worried about him, but he is old enough to make his own decisions.
4. The teacher can refer the young man to his minister, football coach, or other counselor.

GRANDPARENTS TRY TO RUN TEENAGER'S LIFE

Background

Terry, a senior, has just turned 18. She and another girl have decided to move out of their homes and rent a trailer. Both girls have part-time jobs so that they can pay the rent. Terry's grandmother, who has taken care of her for 10 years, tearfully called the teacher, explained the problem, and asked the teacher to persuade Terry to return home.

Problem

Grandparents oppose a student's leaving home while she is still in high school. Because they fear something will happen to the granddaughter, they ask the teacher to intervene.

Discussion Questions

1. Is the grandmother's reaction a normal one?
2. What could possibly happen to two girls living alone in a trailer?
3. How might the girl's schoolwork be affected?
4. How should the teacher respond to the grandmother?

Possible Solutions

1. The teacher could have a talk with Terry the next day.
2. The teacher could try to help the grandmother see Terry's point of view.
3. The teacher could tell the grandmother that she would rather not get involved in the problem.
4. The teacher could call the police.

PARENTAL CRITICISM OF CLASSROOM

Background

Mrs. Kehoe called the sophomore English teacher to complain that her daughter has been upset by an incident in class. A boy in the room frequently uses foul language in front of some of the girls. Mrs. Kehoe's daughter feels offended and does not know what to do. The teacher has not been aware of the problem but promises to do something about it. Unknown to the teacher, Mrs. Kehoe has also complained to the principal.

Problem

Improper language has been used in class without the teacher's apparent knowledge. An irate parent has notified both principal and teacher, although the teacher is not aware of the principal's knowledge of the situation.

Discussion Questions

1. Is a teacher responsible for everything that goes on in class?
2. Should the principal have spoken to the teacher?
3. Why do you think the parent did not tell the teacher she had already spoken to the principal?
4. How should the teacher handle the classroom situation?

Possible Solutions

1. The teacher should ask the Kehoe girl for the culprit's name and then reprimand him.
2. The teacher should be more alert to what is happening in class and try to prevent further incidents.
3. The teacher should ask the principal for help.

STUDENTS WITH FORGED NOTES NOT PENALIZED

Background

In order for a high school student's absence to be excused, a written note from home is required. Many students write notes and forge their parents' signatures and are therefore excused. A teacher seriously doubts the validity of one student's excused absence, but it is the principal who handles the absences.

Problem

A teacher has reason to doubt the validity of a student's written excuse for an absence but doesn't want to overstep his bounds.

Discussion Questions

1. Is this problem the teacher's or the principal's?
2. Does a teacher have the right to question a student's word?
3. Will this type of rule obviously be abused by some dishonest persons?

Possible Solutions

1. The teacher should go to the principal, explain his suspicion, and let the principal handle the situation.
2. The teacher should speak with the student and try to help him understand the possible consequences of lying.
3. The teacher should call the student's parents and try to verify the note.
4. The teacher should ignore the whole thing because it is not his business.

OVERPROTECTIVE PARENT CAUSES PROBLEMS FOR SON

Background

Joe is a freshman in college. His mother, who has never let him out of her sight, visited her son's former high school teacher to seek consolation. The mother, crying, told the teacher how she calls her son daily and even drives 100 miles to visit him at least twice a week. She does not understand why the son, who is on a football scholarship, does not seem to appreciate all her concern. One other child is at home.

Problem

The mother of a college freshman cannot let her son go away to be on his own.

Discussion Questions

1. Are many mothers hesitant about letting children leave "the nest"? Why?
2. If the mother continues her overprotectiveness, what might happen to relations with her son?
3. How might the son help his mother understand how he feels?

Possible Solutions

1. The teacher can candidly explain to the mother how her actions are hurting the son, rather than helping him.
2. The teacher can try to console the mother and suggest that she leave the son alone for awhile.
3. The teacher can listen to the mother but offer no suggestions.
4. The teacher can change the subject by asking how the woman's other child and her husband are doing.

STUDENT UNABLE TO COMMUNICATE WITH PARENTS

Background

Judy is a senior who has just found out she is six weeks pregnant. She and her boyfriend had originally planned to be married in July, and it is now May. Afraid to tell her parents and not sure what to do, she confided in her teacher.

Problem

A student confides an important matter to her teacher but does not feel comfortable speaking with her parents.

Discussion Questions

1. Should the teacher get involved in a situation of this kind?
2. What might happen if the student does not confide in her parents?
3. Should the school provide better family planning information and counseling for students? How?

Possible Solutions

1. The teacher should suggest that the student get married immediately or have an abortion.
2. The teacher should try to convince the student to confide in her parents.
3. The teacher should listen to the student but avoid giving advice.
4. The teacher should call the girl's mother and tell her about the problem.

STUDENT USES AGGRESSIVE BEHAVIOR TO GAIN ATTENTION

Background

Tim is a large and somewhat rowdy junior from a broken home. He plays the role of tough guy in front of his friends, but his English teacher has observed that he drops his tough act when away from them. The last day of school, while the teacher was in her office, Tim lit a fire in a trashcan which the teacher saw him do.

Problem

A student with many home problems manifests his frustrations through aggressive, unacceptable behavior.

Discussion Questions

1. What are some ways students with family problems might manifest their inner turmoil?
2. If a teacher realizes a student's background, should the teacher try to overlook certain behavior?
3. Is an incident such as the one described an indicator of something seriously wrong with the student? Why or why not?

Possible Solutions

1. The teacher should call the student into her office and try to find out what is troubling him, referring him to a counselor, if necessary.
2. The teacher should send the student to the principal's office for punishment.
3. The teacher should pretend she did not see anything and be glad it is the last day of school.
4. The teacher should call the police.

PRINCIPAL LISTENS ON INTERCOM

Background

The principal has a habit of listening in on classes through the intercom system. One day he decided to listen to a history class and became upset when he heard students talking. Without really knowing what was going on, he shouted at the class to pipe down. The teacher had assigned students to work on group projects; therefore they were talking.

Problem

The principal rudely shouts at a class without knowing why the students are talking.

Discussion Questions

1. Should principals listen in on classes with an intercom system?
2. If students talk in class, should principals be concerned?
3. Why do many principals like classrooms that are quiet?
4. Does silence automatically mean that meaningful learning is taking place?
5. How do you think the teacher felt after the principal shouted over the intercom?

Possible Solutions

1. The teacher should go to the office, explain what was going on, and ask the principal for an apology.
2. The teacher should apologize to the class for the principal.
3. The teacher should ask the class to be quieter from now on.
4. The teacher should calmly tell the principal what the class was doing and invite him to come and see for himself.
5. The teacher should tell the principal to go to hell and take his intercom with him!

PRINCIPAL REPRIMANDS CLASS

Background

A student teacher was in charge of the biology class while the supervising teacher was in his office. As students were working with their lab partners on an experiment, the principal walked by the room, heard voices, and entered. She demanded absolute quiet and loudly told the student teacher to keep the students under better control. The student teacher felt absolutely humiliated.

Problem

The principal intervenes in a class which is being supervised by the student teacher.

Discussion Questions

1. How might the student teacher feel toward administrators after such an incident?
2. How might students react after the principal leaves the class?
3. How might the supervising teacher help the student teacher regain confidence after such an episode?

Possible Solutions

1. The supervising teacher should go to the principal, explain that the class was under control, and suggest that the principal apologize to the student teacher.
2. The student teacher should go to the principal and explain what was going on in class.
3. The student teacher should ask his university supervisor to speak to the principal about trying not to humiliate student teachers.
4. The principal should be encouraged by the university supervisor to take some classes in personnel supervision and administration.

PARENTS REFUSE TO FACE REALITY

Background

Thirteen-year-old Nick is having problems with written tests in several of his eighth-grade classes. He seems to know the correct answers if permitted to respond orally, but he cannot cope with a written test. This, coupled with other indications, leads his teachers to believe that some type of learning or perceptual disability might be the cause. They agree that he should be tested. Such testing requires parental approval.

Problem

A student's parents cannot accept the fact that something might be "wrong" with their child. Initial contact by a school counselor indicated that the boy's mother tended to become very emotional about the question when it was raised. His father, who is head of the high school guidance program with a good reputation as a counselor, was initially a bit hostile.

Discussion Questions

1. How can Nick's teachers convince his parents that a problem does exist?
2. If the parents ultimately refuse to recognize the problem, how can the teachers work around Nick's disability?
3. What can be done to help Nick on a long-range basis?

Possible Solutions

1. Teachers should not force the situation or make waves! Nick is his parents' child.
2. Teachers should ask the counselor to arrange a meeting with Nick's parents to discuss his poor performance on tests. Perhaps the parents can be convinced that the problem exists.
3. Teachers should allow Nick to take all tests orally and put a note in his file to future teachers.
4. Teachers should insist on testing Nick, even if it means going to court to accomplish that end. Nick's future depends upon effective treatment.
5. Teachers should visit the home and plead with the parents to get Nick the help he needs.

STUDENT ACTS BELLIGERENTLY TOWARD TEACHER

Background

Susan and Eva sit toward the back of the room in English class. Scholastically they are average students. Recently they have begun whispering back and forth, and the teacher has asked them to be quiet numerous times. One particular day, the teacher lost patience and angrily told them to pay attention to the lesson. Susan made an ugly face, slammed her book shut, and sat belligerently at her desk, glaring at the teacher.

Problem

The teacher has become angry with the behavior of two students, and the situation has reached a showdown.

Discussion Questions

1. What makes teachers blow up at some things and not at others?
2. If a teacher feels him/herself becoming angry, what should he/she do?
3. How might teachers cause students to act belligerently?
4. Are there occasions when a teacher should show anger?

Possible Solutions

1. The teacher should try to calm down before doing anything.
2. The students should be sent to a place of isolation for the rest of the class period. Later the teacher should speak with them about their behavior.
3. Susan should be punished immediately.
4. The teacher should separate the girls until their behavior improves.

STUDENT CHEWS TOBACCO IN CLASS

Background

Jim, who feels the teacher picks on him too much, brought chewing tobacco to class one day. The school has a rule against smoking, but not against chewing tobacco. Jim sat in class with the tobacco in his mouth, and the teacher was not sure about what to do. He did not think tobacco chewing in class was appropriate behavior but hesitated to criticize the student. The boy's father was in the hospital and the teacher thought the boy was perhaps chewing the tobacco to help him relax.

Problem

The teacher dislikes what a student is doing but hesitates to tell him so because he realizes the student feels he is picked on too much.

Discussion Questions

1. Should chewing tobacco be categorized with smoking?
2. How could the teacher tactfully discourage the student from chewing tobacco in class?
3. If behavior is not specifically prohibited by school policy, should a student be punished?
4. How can constant criticism damage a child's self-concept?

Possible Solutions

1. The teacher could ask Jim to spit out the tobacco before coming to class.
2. The teacher could report Jim to the principal or counselor.
3. The teacher could ignore Jim's tobacco chewing.
4. The teacher could suggest that a rule prohibiting tobacco chewing in school be added to the school regulations.

STUDENT LEAVES ROOM WITHOUT PERMISSION

Background

It was the last period of the day. The season's first snow began to fall, and Paul, a lively tenth grader, jumped from his seat and ran out the door to look at the snow. The teacher, with her back to the class, was writing on the board and did not see Paul when he ran out of the room. The principal, however, spotted him and asked what he was doing out of class.

Problem

A student is caught out of class without the teacher's permission.

Discussion Questions

1. Is it possible for the teacher always to know where each student is?
2. Should the teacher be reprimanded by the principal for a student's being out of class?
3. Should the student be punished for leaving without permission?
4. What could the teacher have done so that the whole class might have been able to look at the snow?

Possible Solutions

1. The principal and the teacher could reprimand Paul for leaving the room without permission.
2. The teacher could defend Paul's action by explaining that he did it because it was an unusual day.
3. The principal could ask the teacher to keep a closer watch on students at all times.
4. The principal could ask Paul to return quietly to his room and get permission next time he wanted to leave.

STUDENTS SMOKING IN RESTROOM

Background

Two students asked to be excused to go to the restroom. The teacher gave permission but became worried when they did not return within ten minutes. The teacher suspected the students might be smoking in the restroom, which is against the rule, so she went to check. The restroom was filled with smoke, but the girls were not actually seen smoking. They were, however, the only two girls in the restroom when the teacher entered.

Problem

Two students are found in a smoke-filled restroom, but they are not actually seen smoking.

Discussion Questions

1. Should the teacher really worry about students who smoke? Is smoking something that most young people try at some time or another?
2. Should schools provide smoking areas for high school students? Why or why not?
3. What should be done with students caught smoking illegally?

Possible Solutions

1. The teacher can refuse to give the students further restroom passes.
2. The teacher can warn students about smoking in restrooms.
3. The teacher can tell students that from now on they will be allowed only five minutes in the restroom.
4. The teacher can check students' breath and send them to the principal if there is a sign of smoke.

STUDENTS FROM ANOTHER CLASS CAUSE DISRUPTION

Background

The audiovisual equipment is kept in the room next to the science class. Each period two or three students are usually assigned to work unsupervised in the room. At times students will poke their heads in the doorway of the science class or stand at the window and make faces. Mr. Moore, the science teacher, has asked the students to keep away from his room, but from time to time one appears at the door, thus creating a disturbance.

Problem

Students from another classroom occasionally disturb the class next door.

Discussion Questions

1. Should high school students be left unsupervised for long periods of time?
2. If a student is considered responsible, should he/she be allowed to work independently with little or no teacher supervision?
3. What might happen if two or more students are left daily with minimum teacher supervision?
4. If a teacher notices another teacher's student(s) misbehaving, what should he do?

Possible Solutions

1. The teacher should speak to the principal or guidance counselor about better supervision of the students.
2. The teacher should talk sternly with the students about the importance of acting in a more responsible manner.
3. The teacher should have the students stay after school as punishment for disturbing his class.
4. The teacher should invite the students to join his class until they can return to the audiovisual room and act properly.

STUDENTS UNCOOPERATIVE WITH STUDENT TEACHER

Background

The tenth-grade English class has a student teacher, Mr. Miller. Three class members, who have decided they do not like him, complained to the regular teacher. They asked if they might do special work in the library or some other place to avoid remaining in the class. These students are among the brightest in the class and have never given the supervising teacher any trouble previously.

Problem

Students ask to be excused from a class being taught by a student teacher.

Discussion Questions

1. What are some problems a student teacher might encounter in the classroom?
2. Is it ethical for a teacher to discuss another teacher with students?
3. How can the supervising teacher help prepare students for a student teacher?
4. What should a teacher do if a student comes to her/him with a complaint about another teacher?

Possible Solutions

1. The teacher can give the students an independent project because they are good students.
2. The teacher can explain to the students that part of life is learning to get along with all sorts of people, so they must remain in the classroom.
3. The teacher can speak with the student teacher about the problem and see what he suggests.

STUDENT INJURED WHILE IN CLASS

Background

Two students began scuffling with each other between classes. When the bell rang, they went to their seats which happened to be next to each other. One student knocked a book off the other's desk, and the latter stabbed him in the arm with a pencil. The skin was punctured and slight bleeding occurred.

Problem

A student injures a classmate with a pencil in the classroom.

Discussion Questions

1. Can a teacher be sued for an injury occurring in the classroom?
2. Would a teacher be considered negligent in such a situation?
3. Why can teaching sometimes be a hazardous occupation?

Possible Solutions

1. The teacher should send the injured boy to the office to have his wound cleaned.
2. The student who stabbed his classmate should be sent to the principal for disciplinary actions.
3. The teacher should reprimand both boys for scuffling in class.
4. The injured boy's parents should be notified immediately about the accident so that they can recommend action.
5. The teacher should put a bandage on the wound and forget about the incident. Boys will be boys!

STUDENT'S PARENTS CONSTANTLY CHECKING UP ON HER

Background
Susie is an only child whose parents are concerned about her progress in school and frequently drop by to visit her teachers. Susie usually makes the honor roll, so her parents really do not have reason to worry about her grades. Susie confided in one of her teachers that she feels embarrassed each time one of her parents walks into a class to speak with the teacher, because her classmates tease her.

Problem
A student is embarrassed because her parents frequently drop by school to check on her progress.

Discussion Questions
1. Do you think that most teachers would welcome more parent interest and involvement in school?
2. Should teachers discuss a child's progress in front of the child?
3. How might many adolescents feel about their parents visiting their classrooms?
4. Why do elementary school children seem to enjoy parental visits to school more than secondary school children?

Possible Solutions
1. The teacher can tell Susie to be thankful that her parents care enough about her to visit the school.
2. The teacher can speak kindly to Susie's parents and ask them to visit after school so as not to embarrass the child in front of her peers.
3. The teacher can ask the guidance counselor to encourage the parents to visit the guidance office rather than the classroom during the school day.

STUDENT EMBARRASSED IN CLASS

Background
Diane is a sophomore who is very good in Spanish. She does not like to answer or read aloud, however, because she does not want classmates to think she is showing off. She asked the teacher not to call on her in class because she does not want others to think she is a "brain."

Problem
A student, who wants to keep classmates from knowing how smart she is, begs the teacher not to call on her.

Discussion Questions

1. What might be the reasons for Diane's acting in this manner?
2. How can teachers help students feel more at ease in a classroom?
3. How can independent study projects benefit a student like Diane?
4. Do you think that students know how intelligent their classmates are? Do they care?

Possible Solutions

1. The teacher can let Diane work on an independent study project.
2. The teacher can respect Diane's wishes and try not to embarrass her.
3. The teacher can explain to Diane that it is important to respond orally in a foreign language, and she will be penalized if she refuses.
4. The teacher can tell Diane that she is only making the situation worse by trying to remain inconspicuous.

PARENTS IGNORE NOTES SENT HOME

Background

Scott is an eleventh grader who is a frequent source of disturbance in civics class. He forgets materials, does not study properly, and talks a lot without permission during class. The teacher has sent two notes home to his family recently asking for their cooperation in speaking with Scott. However, Scott continues his uncooperative behavior and seems oblivious of the teacher's concern.

Problem

The parents of a troublesome student seem to ignore the teacher's appeals for help with their son.

Discussion Questions

1. How can teachers get parents more involved with their children's schoolwork?
2. What might Scott's behavior indicate about his home life?
3. How should teachers expect to handle large classes with several problem children such as Scott?
4. What might the teacher do to make the class more interesting for Scott?

Possible Solutions

1. The teacher could make a home visit to speak with Scott's parents.
2. The teacher should threaten to send Scott to the principal if he continues misbehaving in class.
3. The teacher should refer Scott to the guidance counselor.
4. The teacher should try to challenge Scott by giving him meaningful assignments.
5. The teacher should counsel Scott in an effort to help him improve in attitude and study habits.

TEACHER LOCKED OUT OF CLASS BY STUDENTS

Background

Ms. Reed teaches sophomore English. During the ten-minute break between classes, Ms. Reed went to the office on a brief errand. It was springtime and everyone was feeling in a cheerful mood. When she returned from the office, Ms. Reed found that her students had locked her out of the room.

Problem

A teacher is locked out of the classroom as a joke and is not certain how to react to the situation.

Discussion Questions

1. Do teachers occasionally need to ignore practical jokes? Why or why not?
2. Should teachers expect occasional pranks to be played on them?
3. Why do teachers need to have a good sense of humor?
4. Why are some teachers victims of pranks more frequently than others?

Possible Solutions

1. The teacher should walk down the corridor praying that the students will open the door before she returns.
2. The teacher should beat on the door and threaten to punish every student.
3. The teacher should laugh at the joke and then politely ask the students to open the door.
4. The teacher should threaten to get the principal if they do not open the door at once.

STUDENT TALKS TOO MUCH IN CLASS

Background

Mary is a senior who loves to chatter with her friends any time she gets a chance. She is a pleasant girl and an average student. Her habit of talking to friends during class has become annoying to the teacher, who has tried to ignore Mary's talking. At times Mr. Taylor has stopped what he was doing to scowl at Mary. At such times Mary quiets down.

Problem

A student talks a great deal in class with friends and is annoying the teacher.

Discussion Questions

1. How can teachers quiet students down or keep them from talking?
2. Why might Mary talk so much in class?
3. What might the teacher get Mary to do in order to keep her occupied?
4. What activities might a teacher encourage to provide students an opportunity to talk with classmates?

Possible Solutions

1. The teacher should try to make class more interesting so students won't have to talk with friends all the time.
2. The teacher should talk to Mary privately and ask her to be more considerate of others.
3. The teacher should make her write "I will be quiet in class" 200 times.
4. The teacher should send Mary out of the room until she can behave properly.

STUDENTS GAMBLE WITH LUNCH MONEY

Background

Ronnie and Eddie are eighth graders who come from a very low economic background. The teacher noticed that the two boys are playing cards and gambling their lunch money each day before school. The parents of both boys are quite religious and would be most upset if they realized what their children were doing. The teacher spoke to the boys one day about the gambling, but they continue to do it when they think the teacher is not looking.

Problem

Two boys with a limited income are gambling with their lunch money each day. Because the gambling occurs before school, the teacher is not certain what position to take.

Discussion Questions

1. Should teachers be concerned with the conduct of students before and after school?
2. What type of things can children learn from playing cards?
3. Is the boys' use of their money really any of the teacher's business?
4. Should children be allowed to make a certain number of mistakes so that they may learn from experience?

Possible Solutions

1. The teacher should speak privately with the boys about their habit.
2. The teacher should notify the parents and let them handle the situation.
3. The teacher should collect the students' cards and lunch money each day and hold them until needed.
4. The teacher should find some way to discipline the boys for their behavior.

AFTER-SCHOOL JOB CAUSES IN-SCHOOL PROBLEMS

Background

Jeff is a senior who has recently taken on an evening job to pay for a car. He works from 4–11 P.M. and at times works extra hours. He frequently falls asleep in class and generally appears tired and rundown. His parents are not particularly happy about his working so many hours, and his teacher has spoken to him several times about being sleepy in class.

Problem

A student's after-school job is affecting his schoolwork and health in a negative way.

Discussion Questions

1. Should there be a limitation on the number of hours students can work after school?
2. Should high school students be required to maintain certain academic standards if working after school?
3. Should parents discourage students from working on weeknights?
4. If a student is obviously very sleepy or tired in class, should he be allowed to sleep in class?

Possible Solutions

1. The teacher should call Jeff's parents and recommend that he quit his job or work fewer hours each week.
2. The teacher should speak with Jeff again and warn him that he needs to stay awake in class or else!
3. The teacher should fail Jeff and let him learn the hard way.
4. The teacher should send Jeff to the school health clinic so that he can get more sleep without disturbing the class.

STUDENT LIES TO TEACHER

Background

Jack is a seventh grader who came to school one day with his hand badly injured and bandaged. When the teacher asked him what happened, Jack replied that he caught it in an elevator and had to have stitches. The teacher later overheard the boy telling one of his friends that he cut it while trying to steal a stop sign. The teacher was puzzled by the inconsistency of these stories.

Problem

A student tells his teacher one thing and his friends something else. The teacher does not know what to believe.

Discussion Questions

1. What should a teacher do if she/he finds a student lying?
2. Might Jack have reason not to tell the teacher about the stop sign?
3. Why might Jack have told two different stories?
4. Is it really important that the teacher know what truly happened?

Possible Solutions

1. The teacher should confront Jack with the situation and ask him to tell the truth.
2. The teacher should not worry about the problem since it was discovered by eavesdropping.
3. The teacher should call Jack's family to see what really happened.
4. The teacher should talk to Jack about lying.

STUDENT NEEDS REASSURANCE

Background

Ken is a sophomore from a broken home who lives with his mother who works. Ken is shy around classmates but has the irritating habit of raising his hand and asking numerous questions every day. Some of the questions seem so trivial that classmates frequently laugh at him. Ken makes good grades but appears to need a great deal of reassurance about his schoolwork.

Problem

A student who is obviously intelligent and gets good grades finds it necessary to continuously ask questions. The teacher feels the boy must have a reason for feeling insecure.

Discussion Questions

1. When a student continuously asks questions in class, what might this indicate?
2. How can a teacher reassure a child who apparently needs continual reassurance?
3. What should a teacher do when classmates make fun of another child?
4. Should a teacher try to ignore questions that appear irrelevant or trivial? Is any question ever irrelevant?

Possible Solutions

1. The teacher should make an honest effort to answer all Ken's questions.
2. The teacher should sometimes ignore Ken's hand when he raises it to ask a question.
3. The teacher should talk with Ken's mother to see if there is a major problem at home.
4. The teacher should talk to Ken privately, explain that some of his questions are considered foolish by his classmates, and suggest that he think before he raises his hand.

STUDENT COMES TO CLASS DRUNK

Background

Tony is a senior who enjoys partying on weekends. He is not very well liked by most teachers but has developed good rapport with his English teacher. One morning Tony came to English class obviously under the influence of alcohol. He grinned sheepishly at the teacher and went quietly to his seat. He caused no trouble, but his classmates were immediately aware of his condition. The teacher knew if she reported him that he would be suspended.

Problem

A student comes to class drunk. What should the teacher do?

Discussion Questions

1. If the teacher has developed good rapport with a student who needs encouragement and support, should the teacher overlook certain deficiencies the student might have?
2. If a student breaks a school rule, should the teacher always discipline the student?
3. Which is more important, rules or people?
4. How can a teacher let a student know that he/she disapproves of the action, not the person?

Possible Solutions

1. The teacher should ask Tony to leave the room.
2. The teacher should take Tony to the principal's office for discipline.
3. The teacher should ask Tony to sit in her office and do his work there.
4. The teacher should pretend not to notice Tony's condition and try to carry on the class in a normal manner.

STUDENT OFFERS TEACHER STOLEN GOODS

Background

Tom is a junior from a low socioeconomic background. He lives with his mother but visits his father on weekends. When he visits his father, they usually do some drinking. Tom frequently gets into trouble at school. One Monday morning, he approached the teacher and asked if he would like to buy some packaged meat at a ridiculously low price. The teacher suspected Tom of selling stolen goods when he refused to reveal the source of the meat. Tom also asked the teacher to keep quiet about the offer.

Problem

A teacher suspects a student of trying to sell stolen goods but has no actual proof.

Discussion Questions

1. If a teacher suspects a student of trying to sell stolen goods but has no actual proof, what should he/she do?
2. Should a teacher buy things from students if the items are not school-sponsored?
3. What might happen if the teacher buys the meat?
4. How might an honest student feel if the teacher he trusts accuses him of a dishonest act which he did not commit?

Possible Solutions

1. The teacher should buy the meat and ask no further questions.
2. The teacher should think of an excuse not to buy the meat.
3. The teacher should continue to quiz Tom in an effort to find out whether or not the meat is from a reliable source.
4. The teacher should tell Tom that something is "tainted."

IRREGULAR SCHOOL ATTENDANCE CAUSES PROBLEMS

Background

Philip is a sophomore with very irregular school attendance. He is frequently absent on Fridays and Mondays but brings notes from his mother saying he was sick. The teacher suspects the student of forging his mother's signature. One Friday while driving to school, the teacher saw Philip hitchhiking toward another town. When he failed to attend class that day, the teacher was determined to do something about the note she believed Philip would bring when he returned.

Problem

A teacher feels that some action should be taken toward a student who is suspected of playing hooky and later forging excuse notes.

Discussion Questions

1. How can absenteeism affect school work?
2. When should a teacher become concerned about absenteeism?
3. What should the teacher have done when she saw the student hitchhiking?
4. How do parents sometimes contribute to the truancy and delinquency of their children?

Possible Solutions

1. The teacher should report the situation to the principal immediately.
2. The teacher should call the parents to see if they know where Philip is on school days.
3. The teacher should wait until Philip comes to school and then confront him.

STUDENT EMBARRASSES TEACHER IN CAFETERIA

Background

Mr. Ross was in the cafeteria line waiting to be served. A few feet ahead he noticed a student cutting the line, which is against school rules. He did not know the student and did not want to make a big issue of the student's cutting, so he decided to speak to him after he went through the line. When he passed the boy with his tray, Mr. Ross motioned to him and asked why he cut line. Without speaking, the student picked up his bowl of ice cream and shoved it in Mr. Ross's face!

Problem

A teacher who tries to be tactful about reminding a student of an infraction of a school rule receives a bowl of ice cream in the face while numerous students and teachers are observing.

Discussion Questions

1. What should the teacher do now?
2. What would your reaction be if someone shoved a bowl of ice cream in your face?
3. Should the teacher try to help the student "save face" or should Mr. Ross get back at him in some way?
4. What might happen if the teacher started screaming at the student?

Possible Solutions

1. The teacher should shove the bowl in the student's face.
2. The teacher should try to act as nonchalantly as possible and ask to see the student privately after lunch.
3. The teacher should laugh and act as if the whole incident were a big joke.
4. The teacher should reprimand the student right there in front of everyone.

PARENT'S DEATH AFFECTS STUDENT

Background

Bob is a senior who has an excellent academic attendance record. His father died suddenly from a heart attack. Bob was absent two days, returned to school, and in the following weeks seemed to have given up trying. The teacher as well as Bob's classmates noticed the change in Bob's attitude and are concerned about his welfare. His girlfriend has tried to cheer him up as best she can.

Problem

A fine student whose father recently died has a difficult time getting back into the swing of things. He seems to have lost all interest in school.

Discussion Questions

1. How can teachers help prepare students for death?
2. How should teachers treat children after a parent dies?
3. How can classmates help other students with tragedies such as death?
4. What type of classroom activities might encourage or challenge a student like Bob?

Possible Solutions

1. The teacher should spend as much time as possible trying to counsel Bob.
2. The teacher should call Bob's mother to see if she is aware of the situation.
3. The teacher should ask classmates to try to help Bob.
4. The teacher should give Bob higher grades than he deserves and hope that he will soon be back to his old self again.

STUDENT'S LACK OF HYGIENE DISTURBS CLASS

Background

Willie is a tenth grader from a very low socioeconomic background. He is currently living with an aunt and works after school to support himself. Willie's body has a very strong, disagreeable odor which disturbs the class. Several students have approached the teacher to complain about Willie. Unkind comments have also been made about him during class.

Problem

How can a teacher tactfully tell a student that he or she smells bad?

Discussion Questions

1. Should health and physical education teachers be particularly concerned about problems of hygiene, or should all teachers be concerned?
2. What can teachers do to help children from deprived homes with personal hygiene?
3. Should schools provide shower facilities before and after school for students who do not have them at home?
4. How can students encourage their friends to maintain proper hygiene?

Possible Solutions

1. The teacher should speak privately to Willie about his odor.
2. The teacher should ask another boy to speak to Willie.
3. The teacher should talk to the class in general about proper hygiene.
4. The teacher should ask an athletic coach to talk to the young man.

STUDENT LACKS MOTIVATION

Background

Sam is a ninth grader who gets straight F's on his report card because he makes no effort to cooperate in any of his classes. A bright young man, he is completely turned off by school and wants to quit school when he is 16. He would like to take a shop course in auto mechanics, but freshmen and sophomores are not permitted to do so. His parents are aware of the situation but do little more than nag at home.

Problem

A student, completely turned off by school, sits docilely in class each day, causing no discipline problems as such, but worrying the teacher greatly.

Discussion Questions

1. What can teachers do to "turn on" students to learning?
2. Should freshmen and sophomores be permitted to take vocational courses?
3. How might Sam's attitude affect others in the class?
4. How does the home environment affect a student's attitude toward school?

Possible Solutions

1. The teacher could appeal to the guidance counselor for help.
2. The teacher could see if an exception might be made so that Sam could get into the vocational program.
3. The teacher could speak with Sam and his parents to see what they suggest.
4. The teacher should let Sam work on an independent project of his own choosing in an effort to arouse his interest in something.

RINGLEADER DISRUPTS CLASS

Background

Nancy is repeating seventh grade after being held back because of low grades. She is cute and very popular among her peers and has become the ringleader of the class. Whenever she does anything in class, her followers do the same, no matter how much they disrupt the class. She is constantly doing something to disrupt, which makes learning very difficult for those who are not members of her clique.

Problem

An older student, who has become the ringleader of the class, apparently needs some special attention.

Discussion Questions

1. How can Nancy be kept from constantly disrupting the class?
2. When children like to show off and cause trouble, what might be indicated about their personality?
3. Is there a way that the teacher might channel Nancy's leadership abilities in a positive direction?

Possible Solutions

1. The teacher should try not to pay special attention to Nancy because it might encourage her to continue acting in a disruptive manner.
2. Nancy should not be placed in any leadership positions.
3. Nancy's clique should be separated whenever there is a group activity.
4. Nancy should be given a position of responsibility in the class and encouraged to set a good example for her classmates.

STUDENT ABUSED AT HOME

Background

Tina, a ninth-grade student who is a slow learner, has severe scars from burns received when she was younger. The physical scars have also left mental scars. The girl, who is very self-conscious in a group, told the teacher one day she would not be able to participate in the day's activities. When asked why, she showed the teacher her legs, which were red and badly bruised. She reported that her stepfather had beaten her the night before.

Problem

A student, who feels self-conscious and inferior around her peers, comes to the teacher with signs of child abuse.

Discussion Questions

1. How can a teacher help such a child feel a part of the class?
2. If the story of the stepfather's beating is true, what should the teacher do?
3. Does your community have programs that work with abusive parents?

Possible Solutions

1. The teacher should try as much as possible to help Tina feel loved and accepted.
2. The teacher can give Tina responsibilities, such as being captain of a team, to help build her self-concept.
3. The teacher should report the suspected child abuse to the guidance counselor.

INTROVERT AVOIDS GROUP OR SOCIAL FUNCTIONS

Background
Max is an orphan. He and a younger brother left an orphanage in another state at an early age and now live in a foster home. At fourteen Max is highly introverted and does not care to participate in social functions or activities that deal with the public. He participates in physical education classes, though in a somewhat standoffish manner.

Problem
A student is very introverted and needs to be encouraged to mix more with others.

Discussion Questions
1. Should teachers respect a student's right to remain a loner?
2. Is Max's behavior typical of that of many foster children?
3. How might a teacher encourage a withdrawn child to participate in group activities?

Possible Solutions
1. Max should be exposed to more group experiences.
2. Max should be taken to public places so that he will begin to feel more comfortable there.
3. The teacher should pay special attention to Max so that he will feel someone cares about him.
4. The teacher should respect Max's right to privacy and let him work alone when he wants to do so.

PARENTS WANT SON TO QUIT SCHOOL

Background
Albert is a seventeen-year-old ninth-grade student from a middle-class family. He is a poor student who has failed more than once. His parents want him to quit school because of his age and because they think he is wasting his time. Albert chooses to remain in school but does not try very hard to learn or to make passing grades.

Problem
A student's parents want him to quit school, but the student wishes to remain.

Discussion Questions
1. Why do you think Albert wishes to remain in school?
2. Will he benefit from remaining in school?
3. What could be done to stimulate his interest?
4. Why do you think his parents favor his leaving school?

Possible Solutions

1. Albert could do as his parents wish.
2. Albert could try to enroll in vocational school.
3. Albert could ask his teacher to speak with his parents and try to convince them to let him remain in school.

STUDENT WITH LEUKEMIA NEEDS SPECIAL HELP

Background

Joey is an eighth-grade student who has leukemia. He has been involved in the intermediate band program. Joey's condition has worsened recently. He has lost much of his hair and wears a cap most of the time. Joey is absent from class often; when he does attend, he shows little interest.

Problem

A student needs to be included in class activities as much as possible, without calling attention to his physical condition.

Discussion Questions

1. How can Joey be included more in class activities without calling attention to his illness?
2. Do you think frequent absences will affect Joey's progress in the class?
3. What might cause Joey's lack of interest in the band class?
4. What might a teacher do to make a class enjoyable for a student in this circumstance?

Possible Solutions

1. The teacher should not worry about Joey's lack of interest, as it is probably a result of his sickness.
2. The teacher should make Joey feel welcome when he comes to class.
3. Joey should be encouraged and complimented whenever he seems to show interest in class activities.

STUDENT LACKS MOTIVATION

Background

Sixteen-year-old José is in ninth grade. He comes from a family of five children where both parents work, the father as a truck driver and the mother as a beautician. José was given a battery of three tests a year agao — the WISC revised, the Peabody Picture Vocabulary Test, and the PIAT. The latter indicated that all academic scores were at least four years below José's present grade level. One factor noted by two diagnosticians is that José lacks motivation. He is intensely interested in motorcycles, however, and is very mechanically inclined.

Problem

A student seems to lack motivation in academic subjects but has a good aptitude for mechanical subjects.

Discussion Questions

1. How might José's mechanical abilities and interests be cultivated?
2. How can a good vocational program help a student like José?
3. Can teachers motivate a student, or does motivation come from within?

Possible Solutions

1. The teacher should speak to the guidance counselor about placing José in a vocational training program.
2. The teacher should let José work on individualized study projects relating to mechanics.
3. The teacher should give up on José and concentrate on students with better motivation and attitudes.

STUDENT DISLIKED BY PEERS

Background

Anne is a ninth-grade student who has always made low grades and demonstrated a poor attitude in most subject areas. She comes from a broken home in a lower income bracket. She has a few older brothers and a sister, all of whom have quit school and left home at an early age. Anne is completely alienated from her peers. Although she participates in class, she does not talk with any other students.

Problem

A student's isolation tends to make her attitude more bitter, and other students tend to resent her.

Discussion Questions

1. Why does Anne isolate herself from her peers?
2. Why might Anne's classmates dislike her?
3. How might the teacher encourage Anne to continue in school?
4. How might classmates help Anne in school?

Possible Solutions

1. The teacher should encourage Anne to talk with classmates in an effort to gain their friendship.
2. Anne should be encouraged in her schoolwork by her teacher.
3. The teacher should speak with Anne privately and try to help her look at herself and the problem she is creating.
4. The teacher should not worry about Anne since she will probably drop out of school soon anyway.

STUDENT HAS GRAMMAR PROBLEM

Background

Joseph is a bright student with a pleasant personality who has led an exciting life. His family has traveled throughout the world as a result of his father's military career. Because of frequent moves, Joseph has fallen behind in English grammar. Even though he wants to learn, he seems to get further behind each day. His parents are concerned and willing to cooperate.

Problem

Because a student has changed schools frequently, he has fallen behind in English grammar.

Discussion Questions

1. How might a student fall behind when changing from school to school?
2. Is it too late for Joseph to catch up and learn grammar?
3. What might be the best way to help Joseph catch up with his schoolwork?
4. What are some advantages of moving throughout the world as a child?

Possible Solutions

1. A tutor should be hired to help Joseph with his work.
2. The parents should be encouraged to help Joseph at home as much as possible.
3. The teacher should spend extra time helping Joseph before and after school.
4. A student with good grades in English should be encouraged to help Joseph during study hall and in English class.

ABUSED STUDENT PUNISHED FOR TRUANCY

Background

Wilma, a seventeen-year-old from a low socioeconomic background, is an average student who has never created any problems in school. One day she ran away from home, was caught by the police, and was returned to her mother and stepfather. Since she was absent from school for two days with no valid excuse, she was suspended for three days upon her return to the high school. Two of her friends, who confided in the teacher, said that Wilma ran away because her stepfather tried to rape her.

Problem

A student is punished by the school system for doing something to protect herself from sexual abuse by her stepfather.

Discussion Questions

1. Are students frequently treated unjustly by school authorities, or is this merely an isolated case?
2. Are there alternatives to suspension?
3. What should a teacher do if he/she suspects child abuse?
4. What can a teacher do for a student in such circumstances?

Possible Solutions

1. The teacher can confide in the principal so that Wilma's suspension can be struck from the record.
2. The teacher can report the suspected child abuse case to the proper authorities.

STUDENT'S FAMILY GOING THROUGH DIVORCE

Background

Don, an eleventh grader, has been very quiet and withdrawn recently. He fails to do his work and does not act as he normally did. When questioned by his teacher, Don explained that his parents have separated and he has chosen to stay with his father although he loves his mother equally. Don feels a responsibility to his family and has taken an after-school job to help support his father, who is now out of work.

Problem

A student is torn between both parents and feels a responsibility to them financially and spiritually.

Discussion Questions

1. How does divorce often affect children?
2. How can teachers show concern for children from broken homes?
3. Is there anything the teacher can do to let the parents know what Don is going through?

Possible Solutions

1. The teacher can be available whenever Don needs someone to listen to him and be supportive.
2. Don can be referred to a guidance counselor who can work with him on a one-to-one basis.
3. The teacher can speak to the parents and try to help them understand Don's problem.

STUDENT OBSESSED WITH GRADES

Background

Chris is a tenth grader whose older brother graduated from high school two years ago. Because his father is a doctor, the family has a certain degree of status in the community. Chris, who has been known to cheat on occasion, usually does the minimum work possible but expects good grades. He often hassles teachers for one or two points on a test or report card. If a teacher refuses to "give" him a point or two, he becomes sullen and belligerent at times.

Problem

Because his older brother graduated with honors, a student is overly concerned with grades and feels he must live up to the brother's image.

Discussion Questions

1. What should a teacher do when he/she realizes a student is obsessed with grades?
2. How can cheating be discouraged?
3. Do grades encourage cheating?
4. How do teachers cause students to live up to the images of older siblings?

Possible Solutions

1. The teacher could speak with Chris about his attitude toward grades.
2. The class as a whole could discuss grades, cheating, and academics.
3. The teacher could speak with Chris's parents and suggest they try to help him change his attitude by their example.
4. Chris could be referred to the guidance counselor for help.

STUDENTS EXHIBIT RACISM

Background

A black student and a white student began to argue in class while other students looked on and started to take sides. The black student called the white student a "honkey," and the white student called the other a "nigger." The teacher intervened.

Problem

Two students begin to fight and insult each other with racial slurs.

Discussion Questions

1. How should teachers handle racial conflicts?
2. How can teachers help students of different races and cultures get along better with each other?
3. How can teachers deal with prejudice in the classroom?
4. Is it occasionally healthy to let students argue or fight things out? Why or why not?

Possible Solutions

1. The teacher could march over to the two boys and separate them immediately.
2. The teacher could call for help.
3. The teacher could quietly try to get the boys to separate and then attempt to find the source of the conflict.
4. The teacher could do a series of values clarification exercises in an attempt to clear the air and aid in understanding.

FREQUENT TARDINESS DISRUPTS CLASS

Background

Harry is an eighth grader who has been late to his first-period class three times in one month. The teacher has said little to him, but the fourth time he arrives late, the teacher is determined to find out the problem. Harry does not seem to be upset about arriving late, but he disrupts the class when he enters the room after class has begun.

Problem

A student's frequent tardiness disrupts class and has the teacher worried.

Discussion Questions

1. What might be the cause of Harry's frequent tardiness?
2. Should children be penalized for tardiness if it is the fault of their parents?
3. Should teachers reprimand tardy students or welcome them to school?
4. Why is it important for a teacher to discover the reason(s) for a student's frequent tardiness.

Possible Solutions

1. The teacher could reprimand Harry in front of his classmates.
2. The teacher could call Harry's home and talk with his parents about his tardiness.
3. The teacher could talk to Harry to see if there is a valid reason for his recent tardiness.
4. The teacher could ask the truant officer or guidance counselor to try to find out why Harry is tardy so often.

STUDENT USES PROFANITY IN CLASSROOM

Background
While Mr. Smith was standing in the doorway between classes, two eighth graders entered the room and took their seats. As the two boys were talking, Mr. Smith overheard one of them swear rather loudly when a third classmate stepped on his foot. Mr. Smith has often told his students he does not wish to hear profanity in his classes.

Problem
A teacher overhears a student using profanity after a classmate steps on his foot.

Discussion Questions
1. Why should teachers expect students to refrain from using profanity in class?
2. Is a teacher being realistic to expect students to refrain from using profanity occasionally?
3. If a student is suddenly suprised or injured, should a teacher overlook any profanity that might follow?
4. Do you think that television has any effect on the language used by today's young people?

Possible Solutions
1. The teacher could reprimand the student for swearing.
2. The teacher could pretend not to have heard the student swearing.
3. The teacher could have the student write "I will not swear in class" one hundred times.
4. The teacher could take the student aside and ask him to be more careful about his vocabulary.

STUDENT WEARS INAPPROPRIATE CLOTHING

Background
Mr. Myers, the eighth-grade science teacher, noticed that one of his students came to school dressed in a blouse which allowed her midriff to show. School policy forbids the wearing of such apparel, and Mr. Myers encourages his students to abide by the dress code. At the same time, he wished to be tactful about the situation. It was the last week of school.

Problem
A male teacher is concerned about calling a female student's attention to a violation of the dress code.

Discussion Questions

1. Are dress codes somewhat outdated these days?
2. Who should be responsible for writing dress codes?
3. Can you see logical reasons for certain dress regulations?
4. If you were a teacher, how would you handle this situation?

Possible Solutions

1. Mr. Myers could call the student aside and explain that her dress is not appropriate for school, although it may be for after school.
2. Mr. Myers could send the student to the counselor, who would then send her home to change clothes.
3. Mr. Myers could explain that he did not write the dress code, but he does need to enforce it. Therefore, the student must go home to change clothes.
4. Mr. Myers could lead a class discussion on the need for dress codes.
5. Mr. Myers could pretend not to notice the blouse since it is the last week of school.

STUDENTS WRITE GRAFFITI ON THE WALLS

Background

After class one day Ms. Robinson, the eighth-grade physical education teacher, caught two girls writing on the bathroom walls. Since several other students were present at the time, Ms. Robinson wanted to be certain she could handle the situation in a positive manner.

Problem

A teacher wishes to reprimand two students caught writing on the walls, and hopes, at the same time, to approach the problem in a positive way.

Discussion Questions

1. Is there a difference between malicious destructiveness of school property and writing on walls and desks?
2. What can teachers do to let students write graffiti in an acceptable location?
3. Why do you think students write on walls and desks?
4. How can a teacher show disapproval of an action without embarrassing a student in front of peers?

Possible Solutions

1. The teacher should ask the girls to remain after class to wash off the walls.
2. The teacher should lecture the students about not being destructive of school property.
3. The teacher should establish a special bulletin board where students are encouraged to write what they want without fear of punishment.

STUTTERER NEEDS SPECIAL ATTENTION

Background

Alice is an industrious, reliable, courteous, and extremely likable student. She needs close supervision and special education classes, however, because she stutters very badly. She is a tenth grader who does very well in school unless assignments are timed. Because of her speech impediment, she has trouble communicating with the teacher. Since she rarely finishes on time in typing class, it is difficult to assign a grade to her in relation to other students.

Problem

Because of a physical handicap, a student is not able to do the work other students are doing. The teacher is concerned about assigning a grade, because the student puts forth a great deal of effort.

Discussion Questions

1. How can Alice be assigned a grade?
2. How can the teacher deal with Alice without appearing to give her special treatment?
3. Should the teacher grade Alice in relation to other students or in relation to her own rate of progress?

Possible Solutions

1. The teacher should ignore the time and grade Alice on quality, not quantity.
2. The teacher should grade Alice on achievement and progress rather than on speed.
3. The teacher should help Alice in a discreet manner, making positive comments about her work whenever possible.

VIEWPOINT

STUDENTS—ALLY OR ADVERSARY?

While the classroom teacher plays the key role in managing the learning environment, students can help in ensuring an orderly classroom. Walter Doyle (1986, p. 424) contends that, "In classes, in which students are inclined to cooperate and are capable of doing the work and in which the teacher is skillful in establishing and protecting the primary vector of action, order is readily achieved."

Your Viewpoint: How might a teacher enlist the support of students in maintaining an orderly classroom?

Contributed by Dr. Hugh Strawn, Assistant Professor of Special Education—Behavior Disorders, Southwest Missouri State University, Springfield, Mo.

References for Second Edition

Bellon, Jerry J.; Doak, E. Dale; and Handler, Janet R. *A Study of School Discipline in Tennessee*. Knoxville: Univ. of Tennessee Press, 1979.

Brophy, Jere E., and Evertson, Carolyn M. *Learning from Teaching: A Developmental Perspective*. Boston: Allyn and Bacon, 1976.

Carruthers, S. and Young, A. "Preference of Condition Concerning Time in Learning Environment of Rural Versus City Eighth Grade Students." *Learning Styles Network Newsletter*, 1980.

Castaneda, Alfredo. "Persisting Ideological Issues of Assimilation in America: Implications for Assessment Practices in Psychology and Education." In *Education for 1984 and After*, edited by Paul A. Olsen, Larry Freeman, and James Bowman. Lincoln, Nebr.: Nebraska Curriculum Development Center, 1972.

Cobb, Lyman. *Corporal Punishment*. New York: Mark H. Newman and Co., 1847.

Conant, James B. *Slums and Suburbs*. New York: McGraw-Hill, 1961.

Doyle, Walter. "Classroom Organization and Management." In *Handbook of Research on Teaching*. 3d ed., edited by Merlin C. Wittrock. New York: Macmillan Publishing Company, 1986.

Dubelle, Stanley T., Jr., and Hoffman, Carol M. *Misbehavin': Solving the Disciplinary Puzzle for Educators*. Lancaster, Pa.: Technomic Publishing Co., 1984.

Duffy, Barbara. "Learning—Oklahoma Style." *Journal of Children and Youth* (Spring 1985).

Dunn, Kenneth J. "What Administrators Should Know About Learning Styles." *Catalyst* (Spring 1982).

Engelmann, S. *Preventing Failure in the Primary Grades*. Chicago: Science Research Associates, Inc., 1969.

Erikson, Erik H. *Childhood and Society*. New York: W. W. Norton and Co., 1950.

Faust, Naomi F. *Discipline and the Classroom Teacher*. Port Washington, N.Y.: Dunellen Publishing Co., 1977.

Gallup, George H. "The 17th Annual Gallup Poll." *Phi Delta Kappan* 67, no. 1 (September 1985): 35–47.

Gesell, Arnold, and Ilg, Frances L. *The Child from Five to Ten*. New York: Harper and Row, 1946.

Gilligan, John J. "The Invisible Urban Appalachian." *Appalachia* 8, no. 5 (April–May 1974): 24–31.

Glasser, William. *Schools Without Failure*. New York: Harper and Row, 1969.

Goodman, Paul. *Compulsory Mis-Education*. New York: Vintage Books, 1962.

Harrisburg School District. *Harrisburg School District Code of Conduct*. Harrisburg, Pa.: Harrisburg School District, 1976.

Hart, Leslie A. *Human Brain and Human Learning*. New York and London; Longman, 1983.

Havighurst, Robert J. *Developmental Tasks and Education*. New York: David McKay Co., 1962.

Holt, John. *How Children Fail.* New York: Pitman Publishing Corp., 1964.

Johnson, Kay. "Flower Mound: A Bed of Roses or a Thorn in the Side!" *Learner in the Process* (Spring 1986).

Kohl, Herbert R. *The Open Classroom.* New York: Vintage Books, 1969.

———. *Thirty-six Children.* New York: Signet, 1968.

Kounin, Jacob S. *Discipline and Group Management in Classrooms.* New York: Holt, Rhinehart and Winston, 1970.

Kozol, Jonathan. *Death at an Early Age.* Boston: Houghton Mifflin Co. 1967.

———. "Illiterate America." Speech delivered at Kutztown University, Kutztown, Pa. on October 25, 1985.

Mann, Horace. "Lectures on Education." In *American Education: Its Men, Institutions, and Ideas,* Ser. 1, edited by Lawrence A. Cremin, and Frederick A. Barnard. New York: Arno Press, 1969. (Reprint of 1855 ed.)

Maslow, Abraham, H. ed. *Motivation and Personality.* 2d ed. New York: Harper and Row, 1970.

Mendler, Allen N., and Curwin, Richard L. *Taking Charge in the Classroom: A Practical Guide to Effective Discipline.* Reston, Va.: Reston Publishing Co., Inc., 1983.

Moriarity, James K. "Discipline and Student Rights." *Record:* Kappa Delta Pi 22, no. 3 (Spring 1986): 91–93.

National Education Association. *Report of the Task Force on Corporal Punishment.* Washington, D.C.: National Education Association, 1972.

National Institute of Education. *Violent Schools—Safe Schools: The Safe School Study Report to the Congress.* Washington, D.C.: Department of Health, Education, and Welfare–National Institute of Education, 1978.

Neill, A. S. *Summerhill.* New York: Hart Publishing Co., 1960.

Pennsylvania Department of Education. *Guidelines for School Discipline.* Prepared by the Commissioner's Task Force on Student Responsibility and Discipline. Harrisburg, Pa.: Pennsylvania Department of Education, 1976.

Perkins, Hugh V. *Human Development and Learning.* Belmont, Calif.: Wadsworth Publishing Co., 1969.

Phelps, Margaret, Director of Rural Education Project, Tennessee Technological University, Cookeville, Tenn. Interview on August 1, 1984.

Phi Delta Kappa Commission on Discipline. *Handbook for Developing Schools with Good Discipline.* Phi Delta Kappa, 1982.

Silberman, Charles E. *Crisis in the Classroom.* New York: Random House, 1970.

Simon, Sidney B.; Howe, Leland W.; and Kirschenbaum, Howard. *Values Clarification: A Handbook of Practical Strategies for Teachers and Students.* New York: Hart Publishing Co., 1972.

Time, 23 January 1978, p. 73 ("The ABC's of School Violence").

Today's Education, September/October 1976, p. 20 ("Teacher Opinion Poll: Discipline").

Valett, Robert E. *Humanistic Education: Developing the Total Person.* St. Louis: C. V. Mosby Co., 1977.

Wayson, W. W., and Lasley, T. J. "Climates for Excellence: Schools that Foster Self-Discipline." *Phi Delta Kappan* 65 (1984): 419–21.

Welch, Jack. "Cultural Revolution in Appalachia." *Educational Forum* 41, no. 1 (November 1976): 21–29.

Wright, Una. "Portrait of an Appalachian." *Appalachia* 8, no. 5 (April–May 1975): 40–41.

Appendix for Second Edition

Included herein are useful references and resources as well as an annotated bibliography of materials for classroom management and self-development for teachers and other educators in grades K–12.

GENERAL RESOURCES

Anderson, L., and Prawat, R. "A Synthesis of Research on Teaching Self-Control." *Educational Leadership* 40, no. 4 (1983): 62–66.

Brooks, D. M. "Beginning the Year in Junior High: The First Day of School." *Educational Leadership* 42, no. 8 (1985): 76-78.

Brophy, J. E. "Classroom Organization and Management." *The Elementary School Journal* 83, no. 4 (1983): 265–86.

Charles, C. M. *Building Classroom Discipline: From Models to Practice.* 2d ed. New York: Longman, 1984.

————. *Elementary Classroom Management.* New York: Longman, 1983.

Doyle, W. *Classroom Management.* West Lafayette, Ind.: Kappa Delta Pi, 1980.

Dubelle, S. T., Jr., and Hoffman, C. M. *Misbehavin': Solving the Disciplinary Puzzle for Educators.* Lancaster, Pa.: Technomic Publishing, Inc., 1984.

————, and Hoffman, C. M. *Misbehavin': Solving More of the Disciplinary Puzzle for Educators.* Lancaster, Pa.: Technomic Publishing, Inc., 1986.

Duke, D. L., ed. *Classroom Management.* 78th Yearbook of the National Society for the Study of Education, Part 2. Chicago: Univ. of Chicago Press, 1979.

————, and Meckel, A. M. *Teacher's Guide to Classroom Management.* New York: Random House, 1984.

Howe, L. W., and Howe, M. M. *Personalizing Education: Values Clarification and Beyond.* New York: Hart Publishing Co., 1975.

Jones, V. F., and Jones L. S. *Comprehensive Classroom Management.* Boston.: Allyn and Bacon, 1986.

Kerr, M. K., and Nelson, C. M. *Strategies for Managing Behavior Problems in the Classroom.* Columbus, Ohio: Charles E. Merrill, 1983.

Long, J. D.; Frye, V. H.; and Long, E. W. *Making it Till Friday: A Guide to Successful Classroom Management.* Princeton, N.J.: Princeton Book Co., 1985.

Miller, J. P. *Humanizing the Classroom: Models of Teaching in Affective Education.* New York: Praeger Publishers, 1976.

Sabatino, D. A.; Sabatino, A. C.; and Mann, L. *Discipline and Behavioral Management.* Rockville, Md.: Aspen Systems, 1983.

Tanner, L. N. *Classroom Discipline for Effective Teaching and Learning.* New York: Holt, Rinehart and Winston, 1978.

SELECTED RESOURCE MATERIALS FOR SELF-DEVELOPMENT, DISCIPLINE, AND CLASSROOM MANAGEMENT

General References

Raths, Louis E.; Harmin, Merrill; and Simon, Sidney. *Values and Teaching: Working with Values in the Classroom.* Columbus, Ohio: Charles E. Merill Publishing Co., 1966.
> A classic text in the area of values education. Presents the theory of values, educational methods for values clarification, and guidelines for using values clarification techniques in the classroom.

Shaftel, Fannie R., and Shaftel, George. *Role-Playing for Social Values: Decision-Making in the Social Studies.* Englewood Cliffs, N.J.: Prentice-Hall, 1967.
> A classic text in the area of role-playing or sociodrama. Presents theory and specific instructions for utilizing this technique. Includes numerous open-ended stories appropriate for grades 4–6. The technique could be adapted for grades 7–12.

Simon, Sidney B.; Howe, Leland W.; and Kirschenbaum, Howard. *Values Clarification: A Handbook of Practical Strategies for Teachers and Students.* New York: Hart Publishing Co., 1972.
> Presents a rationale for values education and 79 specific strategies to help students develop valuing processes. Strategies can be adapted for almost any grade level.

Zaccaria, J. S., and Moses, H. A. *Facilitating Human Development Through Reading.* Champaign, Ill.: Stipes Publishing Company, 1968.
> Provides theory and guidelines for use of bibliotherapy as a technique for fostering self-development. A major part of the text is comprised of books recommended for various possible problem situations such as peer relations, poverty, and self-acceptance.

Assertive Discipline, American Guidance Service, Publishers' Building. P.O. Box 99, Circle Pines, MN 55014-1796
> A complete program recommended for anyone dealing with student discipline. The materials include: an assertive discipline text, parent conference book, assertive discipline resource materials workbook, assertive discipline positive reinforcement activities, and assertive discipline follow-up guide. A color filmstrip with audiocassettes comprise a complete assertive discipline workshop presented by Lee Canter.

Discipline and Classroom Management. Washington, D.C.: National Education Association, 1201 16th St. N.W., 20036.
> This program is a comprehensive training program on discipline and classroom management for teachers and parents. The program consists of eight workshops dealing with topics such as: teacher stress, the causes of discipline problems, and specific strategies for classroom management. The components of the program consist of books, filmstrips, an audiocassette, and a guide for planning and conducting the eight workshops.

Resource Materials—Prekindergarten-Grade 6

The Accepts Program. The Walker Social Skills Curriculum. Austin, Tex.: Pro-Ed, 5341 Industrial Oaks Blvd., 78735.

A complete social skills curriculum for handicapped and nonhandicapped children in grades K–6. Skills include: classroom skills, basic interaction skills, getting along skills, making friends skills, and coping skills. The program includes a 160-page curriculum guide and two videotapes. One tape demonstrates classroom behaviors for students, while the other tape is for use with teacher and parent groups.

The Coping with Series, Revised. Circle Pines, Minn.: American Guidance Service, Publishers' Building, P. O. Box 99, 55014.

A series of paperbacks for upper elementary, junior high and early high school students about the problems, conflicts, and concerns of young people. Each set of books has a teacher's manual that contains objectives, procedures, questions, and recommended readings. There are four series which include: coping with personal identity, coping with human relationships, coping with facts and fantasies, and coping with teenage problems.

Developing Understanding of Self and Others, Revised. Circle Pines, Minn.: American Guidance Service, Publishers' Building, P. O. Box 99, 55014.

DUSO-1 is for use in grades kindergarten through grade 2 and emphasizes feelings, goals, values, and behavior. DUSO-2 is for use with grades 3 and 4; it extends concepts developed in DUSO-1 and emphasizes communication skills, interdependence, self-reliance, and nature of behavior. Both kits contain a variety of material such as story books, puppets, and audiocassettes.

Focus on Self-Development. Chicago, Ill.: Science Research Associates, Inc., 259 E. Erie St., 60611.

Program organized into three different kits for kindergarten through grade 6. Each kit emphasizes development of awareness of self and others. Student expression without fear of disapproval is developed throughout. A variety of instructional media is used in each kit.

Getting Along with Others. Champaign, Ill.: Research Press, Box 3 177, Dept. B, 61821.

A program for teaching social skills to elementary school children. The lessons/activities are contained in a spiral-bound notebook and include such social skills as following directions, saying "no" to stay out of trouble, and giving positive feedback.

Growing Up with Values. New York, N.Y.: Parents' Magazine Films, Inc., 52 Vanderbilt Ave., 10017.

A series of sound filmstrips dealing with problem situations facing elementary students. Emphasis on identifying problems, courses of action, and consequences. One of many programs available from Parents' Magazine relating to self-development. Programs are also available for preschool through secondary school level.

My Friends and Me. Circle Pines, Minn.: American Guidance Service, Publishers' Building, P.O. Box 99, 55014.

A program to help preschool and kindergarten children identify problems, seek solutions, and learn how to get along with others. There are 190 activities that include a teacher's guide, a tabletop activity board, dolls, family activities, activity picture cards, and audiocassettes or records.

Teaching Children Values Through Unfinished Stories. Freeport, N.Y.: Educational Activities, Inc., P.O. Box 393, 11520.

The program includes filmstrips, stories, and records that involve students in identifying appropriate courses of action. Appropriate behavior concepts such as responsibility, love, and justice are also explored.

Transition. Circle Pines, Minn.: American Guidance Service, Publishers' Building, P.O. Box 99, 55014.

This program is for use with students in grades 6–9 and focuses on helping students understand themselves and others as they grow to adolescence. The program is organized into five self-contained units and deals with topics such as encouraging openness and trust and increasing awareness of values. A variety of materials accompany each unit including teacher manuals, duplicating masters, and audiocassettes.

Unfinished Stories for Facilitating Decision Making in the Elementary Classroom. Washington, D.C.: National Education Association, 1201 16th St. N.W., 20036.

This text presents open-ended stories for students. Various student problems are presented and explored through discussion or role-playing.

The Values Education Teaching Resource. New York, N.Y.: Guidance Associates, 757 Third Ave., 10017.

A program for students in grades 2 through 5. Nine sound filmstrips develop concepts of self-awareness and social interaction. Topics include fairness, rules, feelings of others, and working out problems.

Guidance Associates also publishes other self-development programs. For example, *Sesame Street Skills for Growing* (K-2) emphasizes self-awareness, awareness of others, and learning to use mental abilities.

Resource Materials—Grades 7-12

It's Your Life. Westchester, Ill.: Benefic Press, 10300 W. Roosevelt Rd., 60153.

A workbook that involves students in activities of self-awareness, establishing goals, and determining values. Material lends itself to follow-up discussions and role-playing.

Relationships and Values. New York, N.Y.: Guidance Associates, 757 Third Avenue, 10017.

A sound filmstrip program for grades 7-9. Emphasizes self-awareness, increased reasoning abilities, and improving social relationships.

Other programs published by Guidance Associates related to self-development at this age level include *Adolescent Conflicts* (grades 9-12), which allows students to discuss, understand, and cope with common emotional and values-related problems. Topics such as coping with competition, jealousy, group pressure, and anger are presented.

Understanding Stress and Conflict. Pleasantville, N.Y.: Sunburst Communications, Room T.U. 7, 39 Washington Ave., 10570.

This program is part of the Teenage Stress Series and presents an in-depth look at the nature and causes of stress and anxiety. The program consists of three filmstrips, three cassettes and a teacher's guide. Strategies for coping with stress and conflict are presented. Other progams in the Teenage Stress Series include: *Teenage Blues: Coping with Depression* and *Managing Stress, Anxiety, and Frustration.*